D1105556

CONCILIUM

THEOLOGY IN THE AGE OF RENEWAL

International Publishers of CONCILIUM

ENGLISH EDITION
Paulist Press
Glen Rock, N. J., U.S.A.

Burns & Oates Ltd.
25 Ashley Place
London, S.W.1

DUTCH EDITION
Uitgeverij Paul Brand, N.V.
Hilversum, Netherlands

FRENCH EDITION
Maison Mame
Tours/Paris, France

GERMAN EDITION
Verlagsanstalt Benziger & Co., A.G.
Einsiedeln, Switzerland

Matthias Grunewald-Verlag
Mainz, W. Germany

SPANISH EDITION
Ediciones Guadarrama
Madrid, Spain

PORTUGUESE EDITION
Livraria Morais Editora, Ltda.
Lisbon, Portugal

CONCILIUM

DOGMA/VOL. 1

EDITORIAL BOARD

THE
CHURCH
AND
MANKIND

DOGMA VOL. 1

CONCILIUM
theology in the age of renewal

PAULIST PRESS

New York, N.Y.   Glen Rock, N.J.

NIHIL OBSTAT: Gall Higgins, O.F.M. Cap.
Censor Librorum

IMPRIMATUR: ✠ Francis Cardinal Spellman
Archbishop of New York

December 11, 1964

Library of Congress Catalogue Card Number: 65-15249

BOOK DESIGN: Claude Ponsot

PAULIST PRESS
EXECUTIVE OFFICES: 21 Harristown Road, Glen Rock, New Jersey
Executive Publisher: John A. Carr, C.S.P.
Executive Manager: Alvin A. Illig, C.S.P.
Asst. Executive Manager: Thomas E. Comber, C.S.P.

EDITORIAL OFFICES: 304 W. 58th Street, New York, N.Y.
Editor: Kevin A. Lynch, C.S.P.
Managing Editor: Urban P. Intondi

Manufactured in the United States of America

CONTENTS

PART II

BIBLIOGRAPHICAL SURVEY

PART III

DO-C: DOCUMENTATION CONCILIUM

GENERAL INTRODUCTION

Karl Rahner, S.J./*Munich, W. Germany*

Edward Schillebeeckx, O.P./*Nijmegen, Netherlands*

There are already very many theological works and journals, some old and famous, others young and lively, others of a high distinction; some are devoted to the science of theology itself, whereas others are intended for those engaged in pastoral work. Yet there is room for new theological studies because there is a new need to which the editors of CONCILIUM wish to cater, and which, because it is new does not intend to compete with or disregard existing theological works.

In CONCILIUM, the authors are concerned primarily with those who carry out the pastoral tasks within the Church. Much depends upon their decisions and activities. Taught by the experience of Vatican Council II, they know that the pastoral work of the Church and the preaching of the Gospel have something to learn from the science of theology, just as this theology has to learn from pastoral practice. These men know that in practice they cannot get very far merely with the theology they learned years ago in the course of their education and training. A new theology is taking shape which may have much more to say to them in connection with their tasks than what they read in manuals published a decade or more ago.

It is difficult to sketch even in outline the distinguishing marks of this new theology. Quite clearly, however, it is deliberately based on Scripture and the history of salvation. At the same time it has the humble courage to confront the new problems arising from the human condition of today. It seeks, on the basis of our contemporary situation, a better understanding of the Word of God for man and the world in our time. A theological insight of this kind is necessary for anyone who, acting in faith, is actively engaged in the Church and in the world.

Written by an international board of contributors, CONCILIUM aims to offer information about new questions and new answers in all branches of theology, at regular intervals and throughout the universal Church, for those engaged in pastoral work, including qualified laymen who bear ecclesiastical responsibilities. It will do so in a factual, systematic manner, carefully selecting for special emphasis what is of outstanding importance to its particular group of readers. The aim of CONCILIUM is to provide those engaged in pastoral work with systematic information on the whole field of international theology (including borderline problems) by an international group of professional theologians and by representatives of the secular sciences for related questions, thereby aspiring to be "catholic" in the full sense of the word.

Accordingly, each volume will contain original articles dealing with a particular branch of theology—dogmatic theology, moral theology, exegesis, pastoral theology, canon law, spirituality, church history, liturgy, ecumenical problems, and borderline questions relating to the various branches of theology.

The second section of each volume will be a definitive bibliographical survey answering, with particular reference to the needs of workers in the practical field, the question of what literature—books and articles—has appeared during the preceding year in the field of that branch of theology to which the present volume is devoted, literature which by virtue of its contents and insights is of importance to the worker who is theologically trained and to anyone who has a general interest in the typical problems of the Church.

The third section of each volume (DO-C: Documentation CONCILIUM) will provide informative articles on points of immediate interest in present-day theological problems. By means of this section the editors of CONCILIUM will endeavor to remain at the heart of the living Church and to follow step-by-step the daily development of theological thinking with regard to this reality.

These three aspects: original articles, a bibliographical survey and exact information will distinguish each volume of the series. The equal share of attention paid to all branches of theology, the selection of international contributors which will not be left a matter of chance, the actuality of the theology of every part of the Catholic world, the fact that the science of theology as such will be brought to bear on ecclesiastical life without any over-simplification—all this will distinguish each volume from any existing theological publications. Yet, through its bibliographical survey it will introduce the reader to these other publications.

Measured against the illimitable tasks that confront the Church in all countries, every country is perforce "theologically under-developed". In this series, the theology of each country will help that of the other countries to develop.

CONCILIUM wishes to bear witness to the responsibility of Catholic theology for the actual life of the Church. In the wide scope of disciplines represented, in the topical selection and objectivity of its informational service and in the selection of its contributors, CONCILIUM aims to be "catholic", modern in the favorable sense of the word and serviceable to the pastoral practice of the Church.

Each of the ten branches of theology mentioned above will

have two editorial directors and an international staff of established contributors. Apart from this, CONCILIUM will contain further contributions from professional theologians, with equal representation of all countries as far as possible.

The title CONCILIUM chosen for this series of books in no way aims to arrogate any definite, official claims to itself. On the contrary, the choice of this title means that the volumes will take cognizance of what the Church's pastoral authority, which was so remarkably expressed at Vatican II, has laid down as guidance for the faithful. Hence, in a special way, the volumes aim to continue the work of Vatican II. Moreover, this series of books is called CONCILIUM because the apostolic work which Vatican II began, can only be brought to its full growth by theologians meeting and working together (*concilium, con-kalium, concalare*), as a service of believers to believers and to the world episcopate. Finally, it is called CONCILIUM in grateful recognition of the initiative of Pope John XXIII which has been so successfully continued by Pope Paul VI. Thus, CONCILIUM, by its very name, is a constant admonition to us of the necessity of a never-ceasing dialogue.

Although CONCILIUM does not intend to become a kind of reservoir for all sorts of contending views, and although it has chosen to pursue a definite direction—the direction indicated by Vatican II—every theologian is free to offer his collaboration. CONCILIUM does not wish to arrogate any monopoly whatsoever to itself. The only criterion is scientific, theological sincerity in the service of God's revelation.

PREFACE

Edward Schillebeeckx, O.P./*Nijmegen, Netherlands*

This first volume is devoted to dogma. As such, its aim is the same as explained in the General Introduction. The need for analyzing the human situation as lived in the concrete present in the light of revelation is particularly evident, perhaps, in this field of dogmatic theology. Undoubtedly, wherever this human situation exists, it is touched and called to grace by the living God of salvation. Thus the existential human experience, no matter where it is found, becomes really a *locus theologicus*, a source from which to draw the religious conviction that pervades life. On the other hand, however, that particular human existence which is Jesus, the Christ, grown out of the People of God in the Old Testament with its biblical piety, is the only authorized source of revelation to which we have access through Scripture and tradition in the Spirit of Christ, guided by the Church's teaching authority. Therefore, the experience of the human condition is in itself not really a *locus theologicus*. It is valid and legitimate only insofar as it stands the test of the *norma non normanda* of the concrete human condition of Christ, the Son of God, as the apostolic Scripture bears witness to it.

At a time when the world has lost its reference to God and is fully experienced as a *world* in its earthly meaning; at a time, furthermore, when man is represented as a *faber suiipsus* who tries to interpret the world, inquiring about his own meaning, in a purely human sense (giving it a philosophical, technical or poetic meaning), the study of dogma is induced to concentrate with greater intensity on its own peculiar task, which is to bring out the nearness of the divine *mysterium* in human life and the implications of this for our lives as men co-existing with our fellows in this world. For in the definitive gift of himself in Jesus Christ through his Spirit, God has made this nearness accessible to us in faith, love and hope, and has made it livable in practice in the *mysterium* of the Church.

The volumes set aside for dogma in this new series take their point of departure from the whole complex of problems called forth by the modern experience of human existence. Their aim is to reflect upon this living reality of God, who by revealing *himself* to man, also revealed *man* to man. Hence, the history of salvation, illumined by the Word of God, is the proper workshop of dogma, insofar as this history embraces universal human religion, the Old Testament, the New Testament, the life of the Church of Christ and of all Churches and Christian communities, and finally the secularized world.

All this is like the *locus theologicus* to which theological reflection must apply itself in order to bring out the divine nearness in such a way as to make it possible in our time to live as a Christian and as an adult person, and to assume the responsibility in Church and world which the *kairos* of God's saving will demands of us. It goes without saying that this undertaking can only succeed if it is supported by a really catholic, *i.e.,* universal, cooperation of all Christian scholars, guided by the charismatic office of the hierarchy.

This charismatic office, however, has the living community of the Church as its material, which is interpreted precisely through positive theological exploration and dogmatic reflection in the service of a truly contemporary preaching. Thus, in and for the Church, dogmatic theology is a service to the charismatic office and a vital organ of the teaching Church. On the other hand, the value of its findings is subject to this same charismatic office.

It is in this spirit of service *vis-a-vis* the whole community of the Church, guided by the Spirit who is active in the Church's hierarchy, and, within this community, guided by the same Spirit who works in the conscience of the individual Christian, that the dogma volumes of CONCILIUM aim to take their own place in the framework of that ministering task to which this series of theological works has set itself.

PART I

ARTICLES

YVES CONGAR, O.P.

Born April 13, 1904 in Sedan, France. He became a Dominican, and was ordained in 1930. He pursued his philosophical studies at the Institut Catholique in Paris, and theology at Le Saulchoir in Etiolles, France. From 1931 to 1954 he was professor of fundamental theology and ecclesiology at Le Saulchoir. His published works are numerous and erudite, among which are *Lay People in the Church* (1957), *After Nine Hundred Years* (1959), *Laity, Church and World* (1960), *The Mystery of the Church* (1960), *The Mystery of the Temple* (1962), *The Meaning of Tradition* (1964).

Yves Congar, O.P. / *Strasbourg, France*

The Church:
The People of God

As a result of an intervention made by the Coordinating Commission of Vatican II, a chapter *De Populo Dei in genere* was inserted in the council schema *De Ecclesia,* between the first chapter "On the Mystery of the Church" and the chapter "On the Hierarchy and especially the Bishops". The intention was, after having shown the divine causes of the Church in the Holy Trinity and in the incarnation of the Son of God: (1) to show this Church also in the process of constructing itself in human history; (2) to show this Church expanding and reaching various categories of men who are unequally situated in relation to the fullness of life that is in Christ and of which the Church is the sacrament; (3) to explain what all the members of the People of God hold in common on the plane of the dignity of Christian existence, prior to any distinctions among them based on office or state.

There was only the briefest of hints of the first aim in the conciliar text. Therefore, it can scarcely satisfy the request made by Pope Paul VI in his allocution to the Observers on October

11

17, 1963: "Your hope that 'a theology' will be developed 'that is both concrete and historical' and 'centered on salvation history', is one which we gladly support. We believe that this suggestion deserves to be studied in depth." The third aim is fairly well-attained, although not to the point of the formulation of a Christian anthropology, an image of the Christian man. As a result, after a substantial first part corresponding to this third aim, the chapter *De Populo Dei* discusses the second aim *De Membris Ecclesiae* without, however, using the term that would have occasioned interminable debates. A paragraph on the universality or the catholicity of the People of God links these two parts.

This initiative of the Coordinating Commission is momentous. The new chapter is important not only because of its content, but also because of its title and its place in the schema. Words have their own value; one can even say that they have their own vitality. The expression People of God in itself has such depth of meaning and such dynamism that it is impossible to use it in reference to the reality that is the Church, without orienting our thoughts in certain perspectives. As for the place assigned to this chapter, everyone knows the often decisive doctrinal significance that may result from the order in which questions are arranged and of the place assigned to one of them.

In the *Summa* of St. Thomas Aquinas, order and place contribute to the intelligibility of a given fact. In the schema *De Ecclesia* the sequence might have been: the Mystery of the Church, Hierarchy, the People of God in general. This would have meant a failure to honor the third aim expressed above: to discuss what affects the quality that is shared by all the members of the Church, *before* examining how they are differentiated by their function or state of life. This would also have suggested the idea that the hierarchical organization represents the first value in the Church, that is, the distribution of members according to an order of superiority or subordination. But the sequence adopted was: Mystery of the Church, People of God, Hierarchy. Thus, the highest value was given to the quality of disciple, the dignity attached to Christian existence as such or the reality of an ontology of grace, and then, to the interior of this reality, a hierarchical structure of social organization.

Is this not the path followed by the Lord who first trained and assembled his disciples, then from these disciples chose twelve whom he made his apostles, and then from these twelve apostles selected Simon Peter and made him the head of the apostolic college and of the Church? Is this not, also, what we find when we study the very important theme of service and of the hierarchy as service in the New Testament? [1] It is within a whole people characterized by service as by its own proper form of existence that certain members are placed in a position of command which is, in the last analysis, a post of responsibility for service.

Only time can tell what consequences will follow from the option made when the chapter *De Populo Dei* was placed in the sequence that we have indicated. It is our conviction that these consequences will be considerable. A wholly new balance will be introduced in the treatise on the Church, along the lines of Ephesians 4, 12, where St. Paul states the place of the hierarchy and the role of its functions: ". . . to perfect the saints (that is, the Christians) for a work of ministry, (which is the work of the whole body and which St. Paul defines as) the building up of the Body of Christ."

Yet, in Chapter II of the schema *De Ecclesia,* the council only partially undertook the work of recovering the biblical idea of

---

[1] See "La Hiérarchie comme service d'après le Nouveau Testament et les documents de la Tradition," in *L'Episcopat et l'Eglise universelle* (Unam Sanctam, 39), Paris, 1962, pp. 67-99. Reprinted in *Pour une Eglise servante et pauvre* (Paris, 1963).

the People of God, which was one of the characteristic marks
of Catholic ecclesiology in the years 1937-1957.[2]

I

RENEWAL OF THE IDEA OF THE PEOPLE OF GOD
IN CONTEMPORARY THEOLOGY

It is not always possible to pinpoint the first expression, the
origin of the ideas, which, in a few years, have won general acceptance. Between 1937 and 1942 the idea of the People of
God was firmly reestablished in Catholic theology. This rediscovery was the work of men who wished to go beyond the rather
juridical concept of the foundation of the Church made once
by Christ, and they sought in the whole Bible a development of
God's Plan. This led them to rediscover the continuity of the
Church with Israel, to locate the fact of the Church in the
larger perspective of the history of salvation and to see the
Church as the People of God of messianic times. This was connected with the rediscovery of the nature or the historic dimension and the salvific institution of revelation, which culminated
in the rediscovery of eschatology. All this occurred at a time
when, thanks to the liturgical movement and especially to Catholic Action, it became clear in a new way that the Church is not
only the institution, the totality of the objective means of grace,
but that it is made up of men whom God calls and who answer
his call.

[2] The idea of the People of God had been discovered prior to the works
of Koster and Cerfaux, as the simple fruit of the little effort made everywhere to relate the Church to its biblical bases and to the Plan of God
begun with Abraham. See the references given in U. Valeske, *Votum
Ecclesiae* (Munich, 1962), p. 202, n. 62. Our own study cited there, published in French in *Esquisses du Mystère de l'Eglise* (Paris, 1941), p.
11f., was written in May, 1937. An English version is now available:
The Mystery of the Church, trans. by A. V. Littledale (Baltimore: Heli-
con, 1960).

The liturgical movement, still in its early stages, and Catholic Action, already well-established, were responsible for a rather enthusiastic rediscovery of the idea of the Mystical Body. Then came critical studies. In a short but incisive study, M. D. Koster questioned a concept of the Church as the Mystical Body (1940).[3] He held that this idea was responsible for keeping ecclesiology in a pre-scientific state. The time had come, he declared, to elaborate a true definition of the nature of the Church which should begin with the idea of the People of God (of Christ), in which men enter by baptism and take their place by confirmation and orders. These sacraments imprint a character; at the same time they are juridical signs that give visible structure to the People of God and are supernatural, efficacious symbols of grace bringing men supernatural life and salvation.

Shortly after, starting from an entirely different point of view, employing an entirely different technique, that of philological-exegetical analysis, Canon L. Cerfaux showed that the concept of the (Mystical) Body was not, for St. Paul, the *fundamental* concept to be used in *defining* the Church.[4] St. Paul began with the Jewish idea of Israel as the People of God to whom had been given the testament and the promises, the knowledge and worship of the true God, and finally, his presence. Christians are the *new* People, profoundly linked with Israel; and their assembly, just like that of Israel, is called "the Church of God". It was merely to express on the one hand the deep unity in Christ of the communities or "Churches", and on the other hand the heavenly existence of the Church, its mystical union with Christ,

[3] M. D. Koster, O.P., *Ekklesiologie im Werden* (Paderborn, 1940). K. Adam sharply criticized this book in *Theol. Quartalschift* (Tübingen, 1941-4), pp. 145-66. Also *Volk Gottes im Wachsttum des Glaubens* (Heidelberg, 1950); "Von den Grundlagen der Kirchengliedschaft," in *Die Neue Ordnung* 4 (1950), pp. 206f.

[4] L. Cerfaux, *La Théologie de l'Eglise suivant saint Paul* (Unam Sanctam, 10), Paris, 1942. English version: *The Church in the Theology of St. Paul*, trans. by Geoffrey Webb and Adrian Walker (New York: Herder and Herder, 1959).

that St. Paul had called the new Israel according to the Spirit, the Body of Christ. This was but a transcendent attribute of the Church whose definition, if we wish to use the word, remains on the level of the fundamental concept, the People of God.

As for his conclusions, although not for all technical considerations, the Protestant exegete, A. Oepke, agrees with Canon Cerfaux.[5] Here there is no need now to present the many strictly exegetical studies devoted to the theme of the People of God.[6] More than one recent ecclesiology refers to the idea of the People of God or is structured according to this term. After

[5] A. Oepke, *Das neue Gottesvolk in Schrifttum, Schauspiel, bildender Kunst und Weltgestaltung* (Gütersloh, 1950), then in "Leib Christi oder Volk Gottes bei Paulus," in *Theoligische Literaturzeitung* 79 (1954) col. 363-8. Oepke shows that, even in Jewish thought and logically, there is a movement from the *people* to the *body,* but not vice versa. The idea of body is a construction, an elaboration, not a primary concept. St. Paul began with the idea of the People of God. This was the subject of his missionary preaching and when he proposed his doctrine of justification. Only later did he move, as to a deeper doctrine, to the use of the idea of the faithful, to the affirmation of Christ *in* us and to all the ethical consequences of *vita in Christo.*

[6] Let us cite especially H. F. Hamilton, *The People of God,* 2 Vols. (Oxford, 1912). This author has an ecclesiological interest. He shows the permanent significance of the Old Testament and its religion, the origin and meaning of the functions or of the ecclesiastical ministry. E. Käsemann, *Das wandernde Gottesvolk. Eine Untersuchung zum Hebräerbrief* (Göttingen, 1938); H. Strathmann, "Laos," in *Theolog. Wörterbuch zum N.T.* of Kittel, Vol. IV, pp. 29-57 (Fasc. appeared in 1938); N. A. Dahl, *Das Volk Gottes, Eine Untersuchung zum Kirchenbewusstsein des Urchristentums* (Oslo, 1941). This is a basic study, too little known because of the war but re-edited in 1962; C. Spicq, "L'Eglise du Christ," in *La Sainte Eglise universelle* (*Cahiers théol. de l'actualité protest,* Neuchâtel et Paris, 1948) pp. 175-219 (*Cath.*); F. Asensio, *Yahveh y su Pueblo* (Rome, 1953) (*Cath.*); J. M. Nielen, *Gottesvolk und Gottes Sohn. Zum Christlichen Verständnis des Alten Testaments* (Frankfurt, 1954) (*Cath.*); G. von Rad, *Das Gottesvolk im Deuteronomium* (Stuttgart, 1929) and *Theologie des Alten Testaments,* I (Munich, 1957); H. J. Kraus, *Das Volk Gottes im Alten Testament* (1958), trans. into French: *Le Peuple de Dieu dans l'A.T.* (Neuchâtel-Paris, 1960); W. Trilling, *Das wahre Isräel. Studien zur Theologie des Matthäus Evangeliums* (Leipzig, 1959); H. Wildberger, *Jahwes Eigentumvolk. Eine Studie zur Traditions-geschichte und Theologie des Erwählungsgedankens* (Zürich-Stuttgart, 1960).

writing *The Spirit and the Bride* (London, 1935, translated into French as *L'Esprit et l'Epouse,* Paris, 1947), in which he presented the Church in the absolute terms of its supernatural existence as the spotless Bride of the Lord of Glory, Dom Anscar Vonier published a much smaller book entitled *The People of God* (London, 1937, translated into French as *Le Peuple de Dieu,* Lyons, 1943), in which he studied or at least looked at the human and historical aspects of this Church. According to him the "Church" means what is sacramental and cultic, while "People of God" denotes the element of life, God's total life in mankind. Our idea, therefore, was taken both in the sense of the history of salvation and as a compensating concept for an exaggeratedly perfect notion, even though a glorious one, of the Church.

The theme is treated more biblically by Frank B. Norris in *God's Own People. An Introductory Study of the Church* (Baltimore, 1962). The Church is this People whom God made for himself, which was in process of formation throughout the history of Israel and was given the form of the Church as we know it through the action of the Incarnate Word and the sending of his Spirit.

German theologians have done most to introduce the theme of the People of God into ecclesiology. M. Schmaus in his *Dogmatik* devotes a section filled with positive facts to this theme.[7] I. Backes earned even higher esteem for this concept by supporting it with abundant documentation.[8] Many other authors could be cited.[9] Let us merely point out the vigorous work of

[7] *Katholische Dogmatik,* Vol. III [1], in *Die Lehre von der Kirche* (Munich, 1958), pp. 204-39.

[8] "Die Kirche ist das Volk Gottes im Neuen Bund," in *Trierer Theolog. Zeitschrift* 69 (1960), pp. 111-17; "Gottes Volk im Neuen Bund," *ibid.,* 70 (1961), pp. 80-93; "Das Volk Gottes im Neuen Bunde," in *Kirche, Volk Gottes,* H. Asmussen, ed. (Stuttgart, 1961), pp. 97-129.

[9] H. Hanssler, *Das Gottesvolk der Kirche* (Dusseldorf, 1960). He does not really discuss our theme. Rather he provides a popular explanation of the actions of Christians in the world. O. Semmelroth, "Um die Einheit

Canonist K. Mörsdorf who follows M. D. Koster rather closely.[10] He defines the Church as a People of God structured according to the type of an organic body possessing members and a head and therefore with a certain hierarchical order. In other words, the Church is a People called together to bring about the kingdom of God. This People of God is structured and organized on a sacramental basis through the consecrations of baptism, confirmation (completing baptism) and orders (which is itself divided hierarchically into diaconate, priesthood and episcopacy). All the members of this People share in the activity of the Church. Here Mörsdorf develops a complete and altogether positive theology of the laity. He points out that some of the People of God are set apart from the rest by a special way of exercising this activity in the triple domain of worship, teaching and pastorate.

---

des Kirchenbegriffs," in *Fragen der Theologie heute* (Einsiedeln-Köln, 1957), pp. 319-35, especially pp. 321-23. Father Karl Rahner uses the term "People of God" in a special way, to denote mankind insofar as it is now consecrated to God, because of the fact of Christ, and in a situation of salvation objectively possible for every man. The Church is called to establish this redeemed mankind in a formal society. See *Schriften zur Theologie*, Vol. II (Einsiedeln-Köln, 1955), p. 84f.; trans. into French: *Ecrits théologiques*, Vol. II (Paris, 1960), pp. 101f.

[10] "Die Kirchengliedschaft im Lichte der kirchlichen Rechtsordnung," in *Theologie und Seelsorge* (1944), pp. 115f. "Die Stellung der Laien in der Kirche," in *Revue de Droit canonique*, Vol. 10-11 (Mélanges en l'honneur de S. E. le Cardinal Julien, 1960-1), pp. 214-34. In his *Lehrbuch des Kirchenrechts*, 7th ed. (1953), p. 25, Mörsdorf defines the Church as "the new People of God existing according to a certain hierarchical order and assembled to realize the kingdom of God."

II

THE INTEREST AND VALUE OF THE IDEA OF THE PEOPLE OF GOD IN THINKING ABOUT AND EXPLAINING THE MYSTERY OF THE CHURCH

Historical Value

The idea of the People of God, in the first place, enables us to express the continuity of the Church with Israel. It at once invites us to consider the Church inserted in a history dominated and defined by God's Plan for man. This Plan is one of covenant and salvation: People of God connotes Plan of God, therefore sacred history. We know that this Plan and this history are translated into a positive and gracious historical intervention. Unique though this intervention may be (this note is essential to its historical character), its object is all men and even all of that creation which is linked with their destiny.

To relate the Church in this way to the Old Testament, is to ascribe to it at once all the values that belong to the biblical notion of the People of God and that determine their religious status:

(a) The idea of *election* and *call* (*ecclesia* and *convocatio*). This idea had been too often forgotten in the classical *De Ecclesia* treatise. In fact, how were the treatises on Predestination and Grace related with the Church? Election in Scripture is not just a privilege, it always involves service and mission. Someone is selected and set aside *to fulfill* a plan of God that is beyond the power of the one chosen. The whole Bible is permeated with the idea of *Pars pro toto* that is also found in the idea of first-fruits.

(b) The pregnant idea of *covenant*.

(c) The idea of consecration to God. The People of God is dedicated to his praise, to be his witness, to live in order to serve him, to glorify and to help others to glorify his name. The

People of God belongs to him: *populus acquisitionis* (cf. 1 Peter 2, 9).

(d) Lastly, the idea of the promises. This does not mean merely promises of assistance ("I will be with you," Ex. 3, 12; Matt. 28, 20), but promises of fulfillment in a tension toward the future and finally toward eschatology.

The meaning of eschatology is one of the greatest rediscoveries of contemporary Catholic theology. This supposes an orientation of history and of God's Plan bringing all to a final consummation. This means much more than a static study *De Novissimis* such as was usually found in manuals of theology. It seems that the presentation of religion primarily as worship and moral obligations, the classic heritage bequeathed by the 17th century, deprived us in some ways of the realization that Christianity presents a *hope,* a total hope, even for the material world.

This religion of reason allowed eschatology to be laïcized. In fact, at a time when Christians were neglecting this aspect of their message, philosophies of history were coming into being (Vico, Montesquieu) that were the preparation for the great modern interpretations of a history of the world without God and without Christ (Hegel, Marx). Confronted by religion without a world, men formulated the idea of a world without religion. We are emerging from this wretched situation; the People of God is rediscovering once again that it possesses a messianic character and that it bears the hope of a fulfillment of the world in Jesus Christ.

The idea of the People of God, therefore, introduces something dynamic into the concept of the Church. This People possesses life and is advancing toward an end established for it by God. Chosen, established, consecrated by God to be his servant and his witness, the People of God is, in the world, the sacrament of salvation offered to the world. By this we mean to say that God who has willed (according to an antecedent will) the salvation of all men, has placed in the world a cause, of itself sufficient to achieve this purpose effectively. Thus, he has sent Jesus Christ into the world, and has made the Church, dependent on him and derived from him, a messianic People formed according to the new and definitive Dispensation of the covenant and living on the blessings of this covenant by the means chosen by the Lord for this purpose. The People of God formed by revelation and by all the institutions and the sacraments of the new and definitive Dispensation of the covenant, is in the midst of the world and is for the world, the sign and, as it were, the sacrament of salvation offered to all men.

The People of God is a people advancing toward the complete fulfillment of its destiny, a servant and witness people, dedicated to the furtherance of its own growth, according to the admirable term that describes this mission in many an ancient text. *Populus* or *populi* are precisely the correct words found in this connection in liturgical books.

Placing the Church in the context of the history of salvation, the idea of the People of God makes it possible to examine the difficult but important question of Israel, that is, of the Jewish people according to the flesh who actually did stumble (Rom. 11, 11) but who continue to be the people chosen and loved by God.[11] The relation of the "mystery" of Israel to the "mystery" of the Church is one we should try to understand and it can be envisaged adequately only in a perspective of the history of salvation; this includes the question of the Church's roots in Israel and the destiny of the Jewish people in the eschatological context (cf. Rom. 9-11).

Anthropological Value

When using the word "Church" in speaking or writing, the reference is usually to the institution as such. Sometimes this has meant, and even now may mean, that the Church is being con-

[11] Cf. P. Démann, "Israël et l'unité de l'Eglise," in *Cahiers Sioniens*, 1 (1953), p. 23.

sidered apart from men, as if it were not composed essentially of Christians. As a result, a distinction is made in some texts between "the Church" and men. This practically places the mediating institution in opposition to those for whose sake it functions.[12] There is some reality, some truth in this. Yet, to speak in this way is to ignore an essential aspect of the Church, because the Church is composed of men who are converted to the Gospel. This aspect of the Church was especially dear to the Fathers. A thorough examination of their ecclesiological thought shows that their ecclesiology included an anthropology.[13] This is why the Fathers so often described their vision of the Church in terms of typical biblical personages (Abraham, Rahab, Mary, Magdalene, etc.), or of some Gospel parable. The Church indeed is composed of men who open themselves to God's call, Christians who live the religious relation with God into which we are introduced by loving faith. The liturgy parallels this and sees the Church as the community of the faithful who walk along the paths of salvation and frequently refers to this Church as *populus tuus*.[14]

[12] Here is an example from the Austrian catechism of 1894 which was repeated in the German catechism of 1925. Since then there have been changes: *Why did Jesus Christ found the Church?* Jesus Christ founded the Church so that it may lead men to eternal happiness. *How does the Church lead men to eternal happiness?* The Church leads men to eternal happiness through the exercise, with God's help, of Christ's threefold function, namely his teaching power, his priesthood and his royal prerogative. (cf. M. Ramsauer, "Die Kirche in den Katechismen," in *Zeitsch. f. kath. Theol.* 73 [1951], pp. 129-69; 313-46; 330).

[13] Patristic ecclesiology might well be still alive in Orthodox thought. During the discussion of the schema *De Ecclesia* at the second session of the Council, we were speaking one day with two friends who were Orthodox Observers, Father Nissiotis and Father Alexander Schmemann. They said to us: If we had to write a *De Ecclesia,* we would write one chapter on the Holy Spirit and one chapter on the Christian man. Then we could stop. We would have said what was essential . . . This is just the opposite of an ecclesiology such as we had known, which was practically reduced to a somewhat juridical theory of an institution, or a "hierarchiology."

[14] See *Ausdruchformen der lateinischen Liturgiesprache bis Elften Jahr-*

In the community in which the Christian works out his salvation and sanctifies himself, he brings to all the benefit of the spiritual gifts he has received. We are here rediscovering the variety of the charisms or spiritual gifts given to so many of the faithful as well as to the salvific action of true spiritual motherhood exercised by the Christian community.[15] Certainly the idea of the People of God most appropriately sums up these realities, but it is only just to recognize that this is equally true of the "(Mystical) Body".

Historicity Value

The liturgy many times uses the expression *Populus tuus* in a context of penance, for example, in the Lenten collects (see texts in Schmaus, *op. cit.* p. 205f. and A. Schaut cited in footnote 14). There, *Populus Dei* denotes the community of men for whom one implores God's help, his mercy, graces of fidelity or conversion. This community is the beneficiary of God's pardoning and saving act frequently with a typological reference to the various salvations from which Israel benefitted, beginning with the departure from Egypt and the crossing of the Red Sea. People of God, therefore, describes the Church as composed of men advancing toward the kingdom and enables us to express the values of historicity.

As Dom Anscar Vonier saw so well, this is the *locus* in the Church where there are failures and sins, the struggle for a more perfect fidelity, the permanent need for reform and for the ef-

---

hundert, ges.u.dargeb.v.V. (Manz, Beuron, 1941); A. Schaut, "Die Kirche als Volk Gottes. Selbstaussagen d. Kirche im röminschen Messbuch," in *Benediktinische Monatschrift* 25 (1949), pp. 187-96: *populus* is found 90 times in the Roman missal; *ecclesia* 80 times, *familia* 12 times. For the Leonine, see P. T. Garriga, *La Palabra Ekklèsia, Estudio historico-teologico* (Barcelona, 1958), pp. 300f.

[15] On this point, see K. Delahaye, *Erneuerung der Seelsorgsformen aus der Sicht der Fruhen Patristik* (Freiburg, 1958), trans. into French with a Preface by us: *Ecclesia Mater chez les Pères des trois premiers siècles. Pour une renouvellement de la Pastorale d'aujourd'hui* (Paris, 1964).

forts this involves. The Church as an institution does not need to be converted. Reform may be needed, at least in some of its parts, if it concerns the institution's very existence or its historical forms. But is it not remarkable that in the patristic period, which may be considered here as lasting until the middle of the 11th century, the Fathers knew nothing of the medieval and modern theme of the "reform of the Church" but spoke of the restoration of *man* or of that Christian in whom the image of God had been obscured.[16] This is the anthropological point of view.

III

INTEREST OF THE TERM PEOPLE OF GOD IN THE QUESTION OF THE CONSTITUTION OF THE CHURCH

The category People of God as it is found in Scripture makes it possible to affirm *both* the equality of the faithful in the dignity of Christian existence and the organic or functional inequality of the members. Israel had realized that the priestly and kingly character of the people as such (cf. Ex. 19, 5-6) did not prevent but rather required the existence of a priesthood instituted and ordered for the service of public worship. The priestly, kingly and prophetic people, the people wholly consecrated and witnessing, was organized according to priestly, kingly and prophetic functions. The whole history of Israel is illustrated and, as it were, condensed and systematized in a passage of Deuteronomy 17, 14-18. 22. In this connection the concept of "body" would serve equally well as that of "people". It is likewise a kind of type or model for Christian realities, according to which these

---

[16] See also G. B. Ladner, *The Idea of Reform, Its Impact on Christian Thought and Action in the Age of the Fathers* (Cambridge, Mass., 1959).

realities are conceived.[17] There is always a totality of members, all living and active, all sharing in the quality or dignity of the life of the body and a structure of functions with a head that gives unity and controls the conduct of all. In a people, all citizens participate in the life of the city and perform specific tasks.[18]

In this connection we have already seen the significance of the chapter *De Populo Dei in genere* in the conciliar schema *De Ecclesia*. Let us here add a thought that is not foreign to this chapter and is related to the idea of the sacrament of salvation alluded to earlier. It is the People of God, structured in this way, which continues the mission and represents in the world *the sign of salvation* that God established definitively, totally, adequately *in Christo et in Ecclesia*.[19]

IV

THE VALUE OF THE TERM PEOPLE OF GOD IN RELATION TO LOCAL COMMUNITIES AND THE UNIVERSAL CHURCH

The subject is treated most happily several times in the schema *De Ecclesia* under two different aspects.[20] The first is the consideration of the local community as the assembly of the eucha-

---

[17] On this subject, see J. Auer, "Corpus Christi Mysticum," in *Die Kirche und ihre Aemter. Festgabe Cardinal J. Frings* (Köln, 1960), pp. 1-23; "Das 'Leib-Modell' und der Kirchenbegriff der katholischen Kirche," in *Münchener Theolog. Zeitschr.* 12 (1961), pp. 14-38.

[18] St. Thomas insists on this point in one of the texts in which he speaks of the Church as People and City of God: *Com. in Ephes.*, c. 2, lect. 5, in connection with his doctrine of the city and its political rulers.

[19] See P. Barrau, "Le Laîcat, signe d'Eglise," in *Masses Ouvrières* 135 (Nov. 1957), pp. 130-88; Father Crespin, "Qu'est-ce qu'un laïc?" in *Lettre aux Communautés de la Mission de France* (Feb. 1962).

[20] In the chapter *De Populo Dei* and in the chapter *De Episcopis,* either in reference to individual Churches or to the priesthood and its exercise in local communities.

ristic celebration. (German theologians find this aspect congenial.) The second is the consideration of individual Churches as representing in a certain way the different peoples and cultures in the Church. Obviously this is a vital topic in pastoral, ecumenical and missionary fields where it is very important to propose within the whole Church and in reference to the whole Church, a theology of the local community as the realization of the *Ecclesia* and a theology of individual Churches, for example, national Churches in their relation to its catholicity.

In patristic and liturgical texts, *populus* often denotes the local assembly, above all, the eucharistic assembly in which the deep mystery of the Church is to be found here and now.[21] Exegetes agree to interpret in this sense the terms used in the salutations of St. Paul's epistles: "To the Church of God insofar as it exists or is realized at Corinth." He might just as well have said: "To the People of God insofar as it exists in Corinth." But it is a People uniquely one that is being recruited throughout the whole world for the kingdom of God. As for the peoples of the earth, inasmuch as they are conditioned by a certain special way of being and possess their own values of culture or humanity, all these plainly have a place in the catholicity of the People of God or of the Church. This follows from a theology of catholicity that can be supported by dozens of patristic and even liturgical texts,[22] and is to be found in the chapter *De Populo Dei* of the conciliar schema.

This chapter, then, seems to contain in one way or another, all the chief values of the idea of the People of God, especially the

[21] See J. Ratzinger, *Volk und Haus Gottes in Augustins Lehre von der Kirche* (Munich, 1954), pp. 159f.

[22] In the writings of the Fathers and often in the Latin liturgy, especially in reference to baptism and to the motherhood the Church exercises there, *populi* (in the plural) denotes the faithful insofar as they enter the Christian community and form themselves into communities. The expression denotes either the Church as community or the Church expanding among men. On this point there are many texts.

value of the equality of the dignity of Christian existence as well as those values that belong to the chapter *De Membris*. The other values that we have just described are suggested or mentioned in passing, rather than fully developed.

From the pastoral point of view, the idea of the People of God lends itself to an extremely realistic catechesis and it communicates an understanding of the Church that is both concrete and dynamic. It can be shown how, in the midst of all the peoples of the world, God assembles a People that is his—a People *of God*. Not only in the midst of these peoples in an anthropological and almost political sense of the word (in this respect faith and charity, transcending all differences, destroy no valuable natural bond; on the contrary, they purify and confirm all authentic values), but this People is to be found in the midst of every population unit—my village, my city, my apartment building, the train on which I am traveling, the hospital in which I am sick. In any given group of people, each of the different human gods recruits a people to serve him: Mercury, the god of commerce; Mars, the god of war and force; Venus, the goddess of love, etc.

The true God and Jesus Christ, his beloved Son whom he sent into the world, also wished to recruit a People to serve them, a holy People bound by the law of a love that is all humility and service. This People is recruited from employers and employees, from men and women, from Greeks and barbarians, but in it, above and beyond all this, is Christ (cf. Gal. 3, 28). This People has its law, the love of God and the love of neighbor. It has its assemblies, its hierarchy, its insignia, its customs. This People is called to give witness to Christ and to his charity. It is a People composed of sinners who do penance and try to walk along the path of conversion. This is a point that many "classical" presentations of the Church neglect, static and juridical as they often are.

Dialogue with Protestants

The ecumenical interest of the idea of the People of God is obvious, especially in the dialogue with Protestants.[23] Let us speak of this dialogue. This idea provides many points of agreement and encounter. What Protestants like about the category of People of God is first, the idea of election and of call, everything depends on God's initiative. Then it is the historicity that it involves in the sense of incompletion and of movement toward eschatology. It suggests less sharply defined frontiers, because it is composed of a multitude assembled by God himself. On the one hand, Protestants are happy to find in the frank use of People of God, a way of avoiding institutionalism with its intemperate use of ideas of "power" and infallibility, and on the other hand, the romanticism of a biological concept of the Mystical Body whose favorite expression is that of "continued incarnation"; just as if the Church were literally "Jesus Christ extended and communicated".[24]

The idea of the People of God, according to some Protestant authors, would make it possible to avoid an ontological concept of the Church, what Professor R. Mehl used to call *"Ecclesia quoad substantiam"*, and to see the Church simply as the assembly for God's eschatological kingdom. This is not a substantial body with fixed contents but the result of grace which,

[23] See Bo Reicke, "Die Bedeutung des Gottesvolksgedanken für den neutestamentl. Kirchenbegriff," in *Kirchenblatt für die Reformierte Schweiz* (1955), fasc. 17; N. A. Dahl, "The People of God," in *Ecumenical Review* 9 (Jan. 1957), pp. 154-61; *Die Kirche, Volk Gottes,* edited by H. Asmussen (Stuttgart, 1961), dialogue between Protestant and Catholic theologians. On the role of this notion in the ecumenical dialogue, Th. Sartory, *Die Oekumenische Bewegung und die Einheit der Kirche. Ein Beitrag im Dienste einer ökumenischen Ekklesiologie* (Meitingen, 1955) pp. 51, 57, 60, 61, 70, 71, 104, 105, 127, 128, 129, 130, 145, 156, 180. See other references in U. Valeske, *Votum Ecclesiae* (Munich, 1962), p. 239, n. 11.

[24] See H. Asmussen, *op. cit.,* p. 33f.; U. Valeske, *op. cit.,* pp. 202f., 233f., 248-9. Criticism by Protestant theologians of the idea of "continued incarnation" is constant.

because it selects, may also reject. Under these conditions, U. Valeske asks whether it is still possible to speak of the infallibility or the irreformability of the structure.[25]

It seems to us that Protestant thought fails to see what the incarnation of the Son of God has introduced that is new and definitive. No doubt it is on the christological level that this inadequacy begins. As a result the idea of the Body of Christ is not given its full value. There is a tendency to reduce the Church of the Word Incarnate to the conditions of the People of God under the old Dispensation.[26] In the dialectic of *is now* and *not yet* that is characteristic of the Church in its itinerary condition, it seems in Protestant thought, that the *not yet* diminishes or overshadows the truth of the *is now*. All this suggests to us that the idea of the People of God, rich and true though it may be, is insufficient of itself to give an adequate idea of the mystery of the Church here and now.

V

THE LIMITS OF THE IDEA OF PEOPLE OF GOD AND
ITS COMPLETION BY THE IDEA OF THE BODY OF CHRIST

Composing his epistle, perhaps as early as the year 48, James, the "brother of the Lord", addressed himself to "the twelve tribes of the dispersion". This is a title that is derived from the theme of the People of God. James, no doubt, was writing to the dis-

---

[25] *Op. cit.,* p. 249.

[26] See our *Vraie et fausse réforme dans l'Eglise* (Unam Sanctam, 20), Paris, 1950, pp. 466-82; "Pour le dialogue avec le Mouvement oecuménique," in *Verbum Caro* 4 (1950), pp. 111-23; *Le Christ, Marie et l'Eglise* (Paris, 1952); "Regards et réflexions sur la Christologie de Luther," in *Das Konzil von Chalkedon. Geschichte und Gegenwart* (Würzburg, 1954), Vol. III, pp. 457-86, reprod. in *Chrétiens en dialogue* (Unam Sanctam, 50), Paris, 1964, pp. 453-89; *Le Mystère du Temple* . . . (Lectio divina, 22), Paris, 1958, pp. 310-42. See footnotes 33 and 34.

persed Judaeo-Christians. But is it enough to think of the Church as the People of God, in the sense of the ancient Israel who might merely have received and acknowledged its Messiah? It certainly seems that the answer is no. Since the category People of God, within its own proper limits, means no more than this, it would seem that, to define or to designate the Church, this idea should be transcended and completed by another which can add all that is new in the Church in relation to Israel, while at the same time continuing the notion of the People of God.

What is truly new is clearly the fact of Jesus Christ and this means that Christ is not only a Messiah, but the Son or the Word of God himself made man: "You are the Christ, the Son of the living God" (Matt. 16, 16). Admittedly, Jesus is "the son of David, the son of Abraham" (Matt. 1, 1; cf. Luke 3, 31.34). This is to be expected because of the continuity between the covenant and the promises. But Jesus Christ, fulfilling the promises is made minister of the heavenly eschatological blessings that are to come (cf. Heb. 9, 11) of which the Law could offer but the shadow (10, 1). He is the Son of God. Incorporated in him, we can become sons like him through grace. We can become his coheirs and enter into the joy, not of a world of this creation, but of the patrimony of God himself (cf. Rom. 8, 17). Granted that one alone ascended into heaven to take possession, that is, the Son of Man who is in heaven (cf. John 3, 15); but if we are incorporated in him, we become with him and in him, the unique subject of filial life and we enjoy the right to God's heritage. The Fathers often repeat that we ascend to heaven with him and in him, glossing in this way St. Paul (cf. Eph. 2, 6; Col. 3, 1-4).

We see how even the program of the life of the People of God as it was announced in the old Dispensation of the covenant, when it is realized in the Christ-Son of God made man and become our Head, means that the People of God constitutes the Body of Christ: a new title that is given to it under the new and definitive Dispensation (*novi et aeterni Testamenti*).[27]

Israel has sometimes been called "son" of God in the Old Testament,[28] just as Yahweh is sometimes called "Father". But this fatherhood consists in a relation of special intimacy and provident attention that is the result of Yahweh's election and his covenant with Israel. This filiation is not a personal or natural filiation. It denotes a particular relation of the People as a People, in virtue of which, having been specially chosen by God, it enjoys his powerful care and shares in his heritage.[29] In the New Testament there is a filiation through the communication of the Spirit of God and through a true participation in the divine life.[30] Is it not significant that, having quoted the typical expression: "They will be his people and he, God-with-them, will be their God", the *Apocalypse* adds, alluding to and far transcending the literal meaning of the words of the prophecy of Nathan, "He who overcomes shall possess these things (*i.e.*, the source of life) and I will be his God and he shall be my son" (cf. Apoc. 21, 3. 7)?

To tell the truth, the inheritance, which here is life itself, has been largely transposed in the course of the Old Testament.[31] In the promises made to Abraham, it meant the land of Canaan (cf. Gen. 15, 1f.). The idea of inheritance, and correlatively that of heir, became progressively spiritualized in *Deuteronomy* and *Jeremiah*. The blessings connected with the observance of

---

[27] See Appendix III, *Le Mystère du Temple*, pp. 310-42.

[28] See Ex. 4, 22; Os. 11, 1; Deut. 14, 1; 32, 5-6; Jer. 3, 4.14.19.22; 31, 9. 22; Is. 45, 11; 63, 16; Mal. 2, 10; Wis. 2, 16-18; Eccli. 23, 4; 51, 10.

[29] See *Bible de Jerusalem* note on Matt. 4, 3 and J. de Fraine, *Adam et son Lignage* (Paris, 1959), pp. 116f; Origen, *De Oratione* 22, 2 (ed. P. Koetschau, pp. 346-7).

[30] Cf. Rom. 8, 14-17; Eph. 1, 5; John 1, 12; 1 John 3, 1; 2 Pet. 1, 4.

[31] Cf. L. Cerfaux, "L'Eglise et le règne de Dieu d'après S. Paul," in *Ephem. Theol. Lovan*, 2 (1925), pp. 181-98 (reprod. in *Recueil Lucien Cerfaux*, Gembloux, 1954, pp. 365-87); F. Dreyfus, "Le thème de l'héritage dans l'A.T.," in *Rev. Sc. Phil. theol.*, 42 (1958), pp. 3-49.

the covenant were promised to a group of the pious whose hearts were circumcised (cf. Deut. 30, 5; Jer. 30, 3). After the exile this theme was repeated by Zachariah (8, 12) and Isaiah (57, 13; 60, 21; 75, 8-9). Eventually Yahweh himself became the heritage of the just (cf. Lam. 3, 24; Pss. 16 and 73). In the New Testament men may inherit the kingdom of God or of eternal life.[32] This is the land promised as a heritage to the humble (Matt. 5, 5). In the liturgy for the dead, this is the light that is promised to Abraham and to his descendants.

Throughout the Old Testament runs the theme of the promise that God will dwell with his people. In their midst he will make his home in the Temple at Jerusalem. But it is not in a material place, nor in a temple made by the hand of man, that God wishes to dwell. His true presence, his true temple is himself. That is why in the new Dispensation, God dwells, as in his temple, in the disciple who loves him, in the Body of Christ offered and glorified (cf. John 2, 21), in the community of those who belong to him.[33]

Under the old Dispensation the Spirit of God was not revealed as a Person. The Spirit acted as a power in the men whom God called to realize his plans on special occasions. As early as the exile, through the prophets Jeremiah and Ezekiel, who announced a religious restoration, an interiorization of the Law was promised as the fruit of the gift of a new Spirit. Mention was even made of a new covenant (Jeremiah) and of a liberal outpouring of the Spirit (Isa. 32, 15; Ez. 29, 29; Joel 2, 28-29). This last text is the one Peter recalled on the day of Pentecost (Acts 2, 16f.). The promise was thereupon to be realized. The Spirit not only acts but he also dwells. His interventions are not

---

[32] The Kingdom: Matt. 25, 34; 1 Cor. 6, 9-10; 15, 50; Gal. 5, 21; Eph. 5, 5; John 2, 5. Eternal life: Matt. 29, 29; Mark 10, 17; Luke 10, 25 and 28, 18.

[33] See our *Mystère du Temple* (Lectio divina, 22, Paris, 1958). English title: *The Mystery of the Temple*, trans. by R. F. Trevett (Westminster, Md.: Newman Press, 1962).

only occasional, he has been given to the Church as the very principle of its life.

The encyclical *Mystici Corporis Christi,* citing St. Augustine, developed the doctrine of the Holy Spirit, the "soul" of the ecclesial Body of Christ, making the bond uniting Pentecost and the cross, uniting the pneumatological moment and the christological moment. The Holy Spirit is given personally to the disciples, he dwells in them, but he is also given to the Church as such, not merely because it is the People of God, but because it is the Body of Christ.

The Church "in via"

Let us consider this ecclesiological aspect. The gift of the Spirit as a principle of life in the Church changes the conditions under which it is possible to speak of sin, lying and repentance in connection with the Church.[34] In one way or another, a distinction is introduced between the Church, inasmuch as it is a certain superimposed reality united to Christ by the bonds of an unbreakable union—spouse, Body of Christ, and the Church inasmuch as it is the totality of Christians who, each and all, are sinful and weak. These we may call with Dom Vonier the People of God. Nevertheless, just as it is legitimate to speak of the Church in the first sense and to attribute to it, under certain conditions, indefectibility and infallibility, it is equally necessary to recognize the duality of these aspects. The Church is not yet completely holy, as St. Augustine acknowledged when considering the interpretation of Eph. 5, 27 ("without spot or wrinkle").[35]

[34] For the first and last reference of footnote 26, see "Comment l'Eglise sainte doit se renouveler sans cesse," in *Irénikon* 34 (1961), pp. 322-45 (reprod. in *Sainte Eglise,* Paris, 1963, pp. 131-54).

[35] "Ubicumque autem in his libris commemoravi Ecclesiam non habentem maculam aut rugam, non sic accipiendum est quasi iam sit, sed quae praeparatur ut sit, quando apparebit etiam gloriosa. Nunc enim propter quosdam ignorantias et infirmitates membrorum suorum habet unde quotidie tota dicat: Dimitte nobis debita nostra." (*Retract.,* II, 18: PL 32, 637-8). Com. S. Thomas, *Sum. Theol.,* III, q.8.a.3.ad 2.

Here we have one of the many and very fruitful applications of the truth in dialectical form in which is described the condition of the Church *in via* between Pentecost and the Parousia, what *is now* and what is *not yet*. But just as we noted above, we must not allow the *not yet* to take all truth from the *is now*.

Let us add a last characteristic of the Church as People of God in messianic times, during the new Dispensation of the covenant. This is the result of the coming in the flesh of the Son of God and of the sending of the Holy Spirit, which makes it possible to call the Church the Body of Christ.[36] Under the old Dispensation of the covenant, the People of God existed in a special people, in the human, social and ethnic sense of the word. Under the new Dispensation, it is established through faith in the apostolic Word, on a spiritual plane that made it possible to draw new members from all peoples in the ethnic sense of the word, while preserving its own special existence and character. Therefore, it is not for the same reason that the People of God under the new Dispensation is spiritual and that it has *its own* social structure and *its own* formal visibility, independent of all purely temporal society, of all human reality of race, culture and power.[37]

Henceforth it is established not only in a new *community* but in a body *sui juris* and in the Church. From the beginning Christians were aware they formed a *tertium genus,* unlike the Jews and the pagans.[38] As soon as the Church could be free, it was characterized in an edict of a still pagan emperor as *"Corpus*

[36] For what follows, see A. Chavasse, "Du Peuple de Dieu à l'Eglise du Christ," in *La Maison-Dieu* 32 (1952), pp. 40-52.

[37] This was one of the reasons for the victory of Christianity over Judaism, which was then engaged in effective proselytizing, but which had to go through the Law of Moses.

[38] Testimony in Ad. Harnack, *Mission und Ausbreitung des Christentums* 4 (1924), pp. 259f.; P. Batiffol, *L'Eglise naissant,* 7th ed., p. 92; M. Simon, *Verus Israel* (Paris, 1948), pp. 135f.; A. Oepke, *op. cit. supra* (n. 5).

Christianorum".[39] In reality this Church was the Body of Christ. Charles Journet has cogently shown that the visibility and the spirituality of the Church grow in strength together and are inseparable.[40] This is a deep theological truth that history confirms in a remarkable way, especially the history of the Gregorian reform in the 11th century when the Church, confronted by temporal society and Roman law, affirmed its own position as a spiritual society with its own law.

The People of God under the New Dispensation

We see how the idea of the People of God, however rich pastorally and theologically it may be, is alone unable to express the reality of the Church. Under the new Dispensation, that of the promises realized through the incarnation of the Son and the gift of the Spirit (the "Promised One"), the People of God was given a status that can be expressed only in the categories and in the theology of the Body of Christ. This is moreover what exegetes have been saying recently, N. A. Dahl,[41] R. Schnackenburg,[42] Catholic theologians like M. Schmaus,[43]

[39] See the Edict of Licinius, apud Lanctantius, *De mortibus persecutorum* 48 (Kirch, *Enchir. Fontium Hist. eccl. ant.,* no. 353) and the studies of M. Roberti, "Il Corpus mysticum di S. Paolo nella storia della persona giuridica," in *Studi di Storia e Diritto in onore di Enrico Besta* IV (Milano, 1939) and d'A. Ehrhardt "Das Corpus Christi und die Korporationen im spät römischen Recht," in *Zeitsch. d. Savigny-St. f. Rechtsgesch., Röm. Abt.* 70 (1953).

[40] Charles Journet, *L'Eglise du Verbe Incarné. II. Sa Structure interne et son unité catholique* (Paris, 1951), p. 8 and following, 40, 44-49, etc. English title: *The Church of the Word Incarnate,* trans. by A. H. C. Dounes (London: Sheed and Ward, 1955).

[41] Speaking of the Pauline notion of the Church, he writes: "The difference is that the concept of the Church in the Old Testament is perfectly expressed by the concept of the People of God, while the Church in the New Testament is the People of God only because at the same time it is the Body of Christ and the Temple of the Holy Spirit."

[42] He writes: "The Church in the New Testament remains God's People but it is a People of God newly constituted in Christ. The Church is the People of God because it is the Body of Christ and it is the Body of

I. Backes,[44] J. Ratzinger,[45] C. Algermissen,[46] L. Bouyer,[47] and Orthodox like the excellent patrologist, Father Georges Florovsky.[48]

Father Koster, whose book was really worthwhile, made the mistake of not encouraging the use of the category, People of God, considering it as opposed to the category of the Body of Christ, because he was influenced by medieval practice. Canon Cerfaux restricted the Pauline idea of the Church to the concept of the People of God and made the Body of Christ as a simple attribute of this Church, inasmuch as it is united and mystically identified on earth with the heavenly Christ. In doing this Canon Cerfaux failed to give full *ecclesiological* value to the idea of the Body of Christ. St. Paul never contented himself with adding the attribute, the Body of Christ to the concept of the People of God, just as he had received it from Judaism. He introduced the idea of the Body of Christ as the essential concept in treating

---

Christ in a sense determined by, or grounded in, a concept of the People of God."—*Die Kirche im Neuen Testament* in *Quaest. Disp.* 14 (Freiburg, 1961), p. 147. (Trans. into French).

[43] "The Church is the New Testament People of God, founded by Jesus Christ, hierarchically structured, ministering to the advance of God's kingdom and the salvation of men, and this is the Mystical Body of Christ" (*op. cit.*, p. 48).

[44] See the studies cited *supra*, footnote 8 (in the Vol. of 1961, p. 119f.)

[45] *Op. Cit.* (footnote 21), p. 327.

[46] *Konfessionskunde* (Paderborn, 1950), pp. 78f.: "The Church is the People of God consisting of the baptized, given life by the Holy Spirit, made visible in the Mystical Body of Christ, held together by the bond of faith taught by Christ as well as by the magisterium, liturgy, and sacramental system instituted by him."

[47] "Où en est la théologie du Corps mystique?" in *Rev. des Sciences relig.*, 22 (1948), pp. 313f., 330f.

[48] "Christ and His Church. Suggestions and Comments," in *L'Eglise et les Eglises. Mélanges Dom L. Beauduin* (Chevetogne, 1954), Vol. II, pp. 159-70: "The continuous existence of the 'Church' throughout the whole of the biblical 'Heilsgeschichte' should be conceived and interpreted in such a way as to include the unique 'newness' of Christ, the incarnate Lord. And the notion of the 'People of God' is obviously inadequate for the purpose. Nor does it provide a sufficient link with the mystery of the cross and resurrection . . ." (p. 166).

of the Church. This idea was needed to explain what the People of God had become since the incarnation, Easter and Pentecost. The People of God *was* truly the Body of Christ. Only thus does it secure its adequate christological reference.

JOSEPH RATZINGER

He was ordained for the diocese of Munich June 29, 1951, after studying at the Theol. Hochschule in Freissing, Germany, and at the university of Munich. He taught fundamental theology at the university of Bonn before coming to his present post in 1963 as professor of dogmatic theology and the history of dogma at the university of Münster. His published works are in the historical field (St. Augustine's doctrine of the Church, and the history-theology of St. Bonaventure) and on topical subjects: *Episkopat und Primat,* written with K. Rahner; *Die christliche Brüderlichkeit, Festerschrift für G. Söhngen; Einsicht und Glauben,* written with H. Fries.

Joseph Ratzinger/ *Münster, W. Germany*

The Pastoral Implications of Episcopal Collegiality

I

DOGMATIC FOUNDATIONS

Before reflecting on the pastoral implications in the concept of the collegiality of bishops, it may be useful to recall briefly the exact theological aspects of this idea which has become so prominent through the ecclesiological discussions of Vatican II. At the very outset, it must be stated that the doctrine of the collegiality of bishops is based on two historical facts.

1. *The "Collegiality" of the Apostles*

The first is the collegial character of the apostolic office which first appeared as the office of "the twelve" even before it became, as a result of the events of Pentecost, an office involving a mission, an "apostolate" in the strict sense of the word. Today exegetical research has brought forth two concepts: "the twelve" and "the apostles", of which the first is older and the latter must be regarded as originating after Pentecost.

Furthermore, the two concepts were not related to each other in the beginning, but were identified only in the relatively late Lucan theology. Thus, the two originally different, even though overlapping groups of "the twelve" and "the apostles" eventually were equated with "the twelve apostles" and in turn became the accepted notion in Christendom.[1] This exegetical insight has not only an antiquarian value but renders possible a deeper understanding of the task entrusted by the Lord to the men whom he had called to be his closest followers. It shows that their office first of all was to signify the new community.

After a history of failures and unfulfilled hopes, Israel expected a final restoration of the twelve tribes with which it had begun and which expressed its cosmic fullness.[2] Christ's choice of "the twelve" is thus an action of eschatological symbolism, *i.e.,* the original task of these men is not primarily to do or accomplish something definite but to be the symbolic announcement that now the "end of time" is at hand; that God fulfills his promises and gathers together Israel as it is to remain forever.

The selection of Matthias to complete "the twelve" after the betrayal of Judas shows that originally, even after the resurrection of the Lord, the eschatological symbolism of "the twelve" appears to the nascent Church as a decisive part of those who are to belong to the closest circle of the witnesses of Jesus Christ. Immediately, however, there is a new task—to be a witness of the resurrection of Jesus (Acts 1, 22). In the call of St. Paul there is question only of this latter function which is now so

[1] Cf. G. Klein, *Die zwoelf Apostel* (1961), especially pp. 202f.; while accepting these well-founded thoughts, one need not agree with the other theories which appear too speculative to be convincing. As regards the institution of "the twelve" by our Lord, one may very profitably see also K. H. Rengstorf, ἀπόστολος, ThWNT I, pp. 424-38. Cf. also the comprehensive presentation by K. H. Schelkle and H. Bacht in LThK I, pp. 734-38.

[2] Cf. R. Schnackenburg, *Die Kirche im Neuen Testament* (1961), p. 30; B. Rigaux, "Die 'Zwoelf' in Geschichte und Kerygma," in *Der historische Jesus und der kerygmatische Christus* (Berlin, 1960), pp. 468-86; K. H. Rengstorf, δώδεκα, ThWNT II, pp. 325ff.

definite that he knows himself called to be a witness for the Gentiles. Thus, the old Israelitic symbolism of "the twelve" disappears and a new additional understanding of the office begins to take shape.[3]

But let us dwell briefly on the original task: the eschatological sign of the number twelve. We deduced from this that the first "office" in the growth of the nascent Church was to signify the new community since the office was connected with the number. The office existed only in the communal union of the group, each individual member had his significance only in union with the others of the group. Two more notes will have to be added since the symbolic meaning of "the twelve" is the symbolic anticipation of the final restoration of Israel after the pattern of the symbolic actions of the Old Testament prophets.[4]

If this is true, then these men represent not only the future bishops and officials but also, indeed primarily, the "new People" that will be called "the Church". This no doubt presents certain difficulties for theologians because without further investigation they will not be able to determine whether any tasks assigned by Jesus to the apostles were meant only for the future officials or were addressed to "the twelve" as the representatives of all the faithful.

It is a principle of Protestant exegesis to accept the latter explanation and to see in it an important support of their doctrine of the universal priesthood of all believers. It overlooks the fact, however, that "the twelve", even during the life of Christ, were a group apart and clearly showed thereby the special position of the office. On the other hand, Catholic exegesis is in danger of forgetting that in another respect "the twelve" stand for the

---

[3] For the Pauline development of the concept of the apostolate cf. Rengstorf in ThWNT I, pp. 438-44.

[4] Concerning the significance of the symbolic actions of the prophets, cf. G. Fohrer, *Die symbolischen Handlungen der Propheten* (1953); G. v. Rad, *Theologie des Alten Testaments II* (1960), pp. 108-11; K. H. Rengstorf, σημεῖον, ThWNT VII, pp. 215f.

whole Church and represent the unity between office and community, which we may conceive to be a new note of the office instituted by Christ. This is closely connected with the last mark to be discussed here: the eschatological character of the office.

Now we must admit that it is difficult to state clearly what this means. In the first place it undoubtedly signifies the end of the old era with Israel's oppression and failure and the announcement of a new and final condition of the People of God. This change was to come not through the end of the world and the return of paradise but by the death and resurrection of Jesus and the passage of God's Word to the Gentiles addressed to all nations of the world: developments, it seems, not immediately evident from the message of the historic Christ.

"The twelve" had not understood this even after Easter as we learn from Acts 1, 6. Only the Spirit of Pentecost made them understand that the newness of the People of God is not based on racial descent but on faith, not on power but on humble service. They thus realized the "eschatological" newness of the last times. Must not we ourselves continually experience this newness? It is a far cry from the old and ingrained conceptions of man.[5]

The declaration in which Vatican II, following the tradition of the Church, designates the apostles as a *collegium* may be considered an interpretation of the community character that was proper to the original office of "the twelve" as shown above. Interpretation here means transfer to a new set of concepts. The situation of Israel at the time of Christ was unknown to the Christians from the Gentile world. An attempt was made to express the original community of the apostolic office in the juridical concept of *collegium*. Vatican II has taken this thought of the patristic age, which—to be rightly understood—must be

[5] Cf. H. Schlier, "Die Entscheidung fuer die Heidenmission in der Urschristenheit," in *Die Zeit der Kirche* (1958 [2]), pp. 90-107; E. Peterson, *Theologische Traktate* (1951), pp. 409-29.

seen against the background of its biblical origin, since the term *collegium* alone fails to convey the fullness of its meaning.

2. *The Collegial Character of the Ecclesiastical Office in the Ancient Church*

We come to the second historical basis for the doctrine of collegiality. The first, we repeat, is the collegial character of the original office of the twelve apostles who only together are what they are supposed to be, namely, a sign of the eschatological Israel of God. One might be tempted to construct the following syllogism: Since the office of the apostles is collegial and the bishops are the successors of the apostles, the bishops are also collegial insofar as their *collegium* has taken the place of the *collegium* of the apostles. And just as each apostle had his function by belonging to the others who together with him formed the apostolic community, so each bishop has his office only by belonging to the *collegium* which is the post-apostolic continuation of the apostles.

This syllogism is indeed a sort of summary of the whole doctrine of the collegiality of bishops.[6] But by itself it is insufficient to support this doctrine because the decisive realities of the Church are not a matter of conclusions but of historical facts. This syllogism has value only insofar as it is an explanation of the historical development of the ecclesiastical office in the ancient Church. This process is the second pillar of the concept of collegiality.

A rough sketch may again suffice. While in the books of the New Testament we find the ecclesiastical offices still in the fluid state of formation, we see them at the threshold of the post-apostolic era in St. Ignatius (d. not later than 117) fully developed in the form which, for the Catholic Church, has re-

---

[6] Cf. K. Rahner in Rahner-Ratzinger, *Episkopat und Primat* (1961), pp. 70-85. I have applied these thoughts in my contribution: "Zur Theologie des Konzils," in *Catholica* 15 (1961), pp. 292-304.

mained the basic structure: bishop—presbyter—deacon; the office of the priest and deacon being collegial, while the bishop represents the community of the faithful. As St. Ignatius states in his letter to the Philadelphians: "Be zealous, then, in the observance of the one eucharist. For there is one flesh of our Lord, Jesus Christ, and one chalice that brings union in his blood. There is one altar, as there is one bishop with the priests and deacons, who are my fellow workers . . ."[7]

To understand this situation correctly one must not forget that this threefold office, terminating in the bishop as its unifying summit, describes the structure of the individual local Churches. This is significant for two reasons. It shows that for the early Christians the word *ecclesia* meant first of all and most conspicuously the local Church. In other words, the Church is realized immediately and primarily in the individual local Churches which are not separate parts of a larger administrative organization but rather embody the totality of the reality which is "the Church".

The local Churches are not administrative units of a huge apparatus but living cells, each of which contains the whole living mystery of the one body of the Church: each one may rightly be called *ecclesia*. We may then conclude that the one Church of God consists of the individual Churches, each of which represents the whole Church. These Churches are marked by the vertical structure which is united in the episcopal summit:

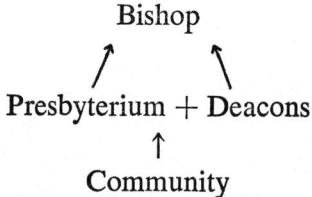

$$\text{Bishop}$$
$$\nearrow \qquad \nwarrow$$
$$\text{Presbyterium} + \text{Deacons}$$
$$\uparrow$$
$$\text{Community}$$

There is a second aspect. The many individual Churches, each of which realizes the one Church of God and yet together

[7] 4, 1.

are but the one Church of God, are also horizontally connected as is shown in the line

Bishop←——→Bishop←——→Bishop

In other words, although the above outlined structure represents a total whole, it yet is not self-sufficient. The structure of the individual community remains incomplete. It is complete only when the bishop does not stand alone but lives in communion with the other bishops of the different Churches.

The individual Church is indeed a closed totality that embraces the full essence of the Church of God, but it is at the same time open in all directions through the bond of communion. It is only through this openness, by being caught up in this network of communion, that it can maintain its reality as a Church. The closed and complete character of the local Church must not mean separation; its integrity involves openness, unity through mutual communication. We might also say that unity in the ancient Church is characterized by the two elements of "catholicity", the communion of all Churches among themselves, and "apostolicity", *i.e.*, the episcopal principle. Here the intimate connection of the two principles becomes immediately evident, for the bishop is bishop only by being in communion with the other bishops. Catholicity is impossible without apostolicity and vice versa.

The foregoing discussions give us an important insight for our subject, that is, while the government of the individual Church is monarchical (even though involving the college of the presbyters and the cooperation of the whole community), the unity of the whole Church rests on the relationship of the bishops among themselves. This constitutes the real essence of catholicity. Thus, the Church appears as the communion of the bread and the Word, of the body and the *logos,* Jesus Christ, insofar as the network of communions forming the Church has its fixed points in the bishops and in their community.

In line with our argument, the episcopal office in the ancient Church is related to the community of bishops, and the individual bishop can have his episcopacy in no other way than in his communion with the other bishops. The discussions of Vatican II and the wholesome necessity resulting therefrom of considering the data of tradition have developed many proofs for this thesis.[8] A few examples may suffice. In assuming his office the individual bishop must ascertain his *koinonía* with the other bishops, without which he cannot exercise his episcopal office.[9] The very fact that he must be consecrated by at least three bishops signifies that he is being received by the community into the community.[10]

Above all, it can be shown that the bishops of the ancient Church were intensely conscious of their responsibility for the whole Church. This led to the many forms of their common care for the whole Church. "He that is called to the office of bishop is not called to dominate but to serve the whole Church," says Origen.[11] The history of the ancient Church appears largely as an illustration of this statement. The letters of St. Ignatius, St. Clement of Rome, St. Dionysius of Corinth and St. Polycarp are the expression of their concern for the whole Church. We must

[8] Cf. Y. Congar—B. Dupuy, "L'épiscopat et l'église universelle" (1962); J. Colson, "L'épiscopat catholique. Collégialité et primauté dans les trois premiers siècles de l'église" (1963); J. Hamer, "L'église est une communion" (1962); W. de Vries, "Der Episkopat auf den Synoden vor Nicaea," in *Theol.-prakt. Quartalschrift* (1963), pp. 263-77; G. Dejaifve, "Les douze Apôtres et leur unité dans la tradition catholique," in *Eph. theol. Lov.* 39 (1963), pp. 760-78. Collegiality was also the theme of a theological symposium held at Konstanz, Germany, on Pentecost of 1964. Y. Congar will publish the reports in the collection *Unam Sanctam.*

[9] Extensive citations in J. Guyot, "Etudes sur le Sacrement de l'Ordre," in *Lex Orandi* 22 (Paris, 1957); also L. Hertling, "Communio und Primat —Kirche und Papsttum in der christlichen Antike," in *Una Sancta* 17 (1962), pp. 91-125 (supplemented reprint of this important work first published in *Misc. Hist. Pont.,* 1943).

[10] Cf. B. Botte in J. Guyot, *loc. cit.* p. 81.

[11] *In Isaiam hom.* 6, 1 GCS 8 (Baehrens) 269, pp. 18f. Cf. K. Baus, *Handbuch der Kirchengeschichte* I (1962), pp. 391f.

mention also the early custom of bishops' synods in which all the more important matters are treated "collegially".[12]

As a matter of fact, the word *collegium* itself appears in the 3rd century as a designation for all the bishops as well as of partial communities within the episcopate,[13] although such other expressions as *ordo, corpus* and *fraternitas* are also in use.[14] This variety of concepts is significant because it shows the insufficiency of the categories offered by Roman law and contemporary philosophy to express adequately the reality of the communal character of the episcopal office. Hence, various concepts were used which, by approaching the subject from various sides, sought to approximate and clarify its meaning. The same search is also of importance for our discussion today.

The lovers of exact definitions wished ever and again to know whether the term *collegium* was to be understood in a strictly juridical or in a less binding moral sense. The former, they said, was impossible because according to Roman law a *collegium* was a group of equals, whereas the college of bishops, because of the office of the successor of St. Peter and the papal primacy of jurisdiction, is not a community of equals.

We reply that it is not a question of a *collegium* in the sense

[12] Extensive citations in W. de Vries in *Theol.-prakt. Quartalschrift* (1963), pp. 263-77, quoted above under 8; cf. also K. Baus, *Handbuch der Kirchengeschichte* I (1962), pp. 397f.

[13] Cf. Cyprian, *Ep.* 68, 3-4 CSEL III 2 p. 746f: Copiosum corpus est sacerdotum concordiae mutuae glutino . . . copulatum, ut si quis ex collegio nostro haeresim facere . . . temptaverit, subveniant ceteri. Optatus of Milevis uses this expression regularly in *Contra Parm., e.g.,* 1, 4, CSEL 26 p. 5 and many more. J. Lécuyer will soon publish a rich collection of texts from letters of the popes of the 5th century in the proceedings of the symposium held in Konstanz.

[14] The expression *ordo episcoporum* appears already in Tertullian, *Adv. Marc.* 4, 5, 2 CChr. I 551; *Praescr. Haer.* 32, 1 CChr. I 212; cf. also *De exhort. cast.* 7, 2 CChr. II, 1024 (ordo sacerdotalis), 7, 3 *ibid.* (ordo et plebs) and many more. For the concept of *ordo* cf. the important treatise by B. Botte, "Presbyterium et ordo episcoporum," in *Irénikon* 29 (1956), pp. 5-27. Citations for *fraternitas* and *corpus* in the collected texts by Lécuyer (cf. note 13).

of Roman law and that there must be more than mere moral unanimity among the bishops. It is a reality that must be defined in terms of the Church's essence and not on the basis of extraneous systems. The result will be a new and spiritual concept of *collegium*. This includes in the office of bishops a community of service and responsibility and the note that the Church is essentially a community of service.

Collegiality must not be taken in a secular juridical sense, much less may it be reduced to the meaninglessness of a mere ornament. It expresses an aspect of the juridical structure of the Church that arises from the communion and community of the individual Churches and the harmonious plurality of the bishops representing them.

The objection that the concept *collegium* cannot be taken in a juridical and consequently binding sense for the Church, only goes to show the inner limitation of this notion. In fact, it is only one among several possible definitions, none of which alone adequately describes what is meant. The use of this word in the history of the Church plainly shows this. It reveals, moreover, that the very rise of the idea of collegiality marks a shrinking of a spiritual understanding originally much richer and wider. A mere indication of the problem must suffice.

In the first two centuries all classes of Christians addressed one another as brothers and sisters in view of the Word of the Lord: "Do not you be called 'Rabbi', for one is your Master, and all you are brothers. And call no one on earth your father; for one is your Father who is in heaven" (Matt. 23,8f.). Accordingly, the individual Church communities called themselves *adelphotês, i.e.,* community of brothers. This usage became less frequent in the 3rd century.

This development is best seen in the letters of St. Cyprian. He still addresses the faithful of his Church as "beloved brothers," but he uses the singular "brother" only for bishops and other members of the clergy. In return, the Roman presbyters and deacons in their letter call him *"beatissime papa"*, and address their letter to *"Cypriano papae"*.[15] When Cyprian, the Bishop of Carthage, and Cornelius, the Bishop of Rome, write to one another, the form of address used is "brother"; but this is now a title of dignity for peers whom the inferiors must address as *"papa"*. This is a first contraction; the idea of brother no longer comprises the whole Church but is restricted to a narrower circle for which now also the title *"fraternitas"* (*adelphotês*) is reserved.[16]

A second contraction or change takes place when the word "brother", which breathes the simplicity of the Gospel and its disregard of officialdom, is gradually replaced by the formal title of *collega* taken over from Roman law. Simultaneously the word *fraternitas* is discarded in favor of the word *collegium* which we find in the 4th and 5th centuries as the current designation for the community of bishops.[17] Also, the other terms that are now in use, such as *ordo* and *corpus,* are taken from the language of the law and indicate the same development.

[15] *Epist.* 30 CSEL III 2 p. 549. I treated briefly of this development in my booklet *Die christliche Bruederlichkeit* (1960) which will soon appear in a new and enlarged edition. Cf. also my article "Fraternité" about to appear in *Dict. de Spiritualité,* where the patristic development is given extensive treatment.

[16] Here again is a twofold contraction: "brother" becomes, first, the mutual address of clerics, *e.g.,* Hilarius, *Coll. antiar.* B.I. 6 CSEL 65, 102; B. II 1, 1 *ibid.* 105; Gennadius, *Ep. enc.* PG 85, 1617 D; Leo the Great, *Ep.* 13, 2 PL 54, 665;—it becomes, secondly, a title of monks, *e.g.,* Basilius, *Reg. brev. tract.* 104 PG 31, 1154 C and elsewhere; Greg. Nyss., *Ep.* 238 PG 37, 380 C; Hieronymus, *Ep.* 134, 2 PL 22, 1162. Other citations in my article "Fraternité" mentioned in note 15.

[17] The title *collega* appears for the first time in the Church in Cyprian, *Ep.* 22. For Optatus of Milevis it is already a commonly accepted title used by bishops among themselves. In his endeavor to emphasize the idea of "brother" he distinguishes in the Donatist bishops *collega* from *frater*. He is *collega* as a fellow bishop, *frater* as a fellow Christian, *e.g., Contra Parm.* I, 4 CSEL 26 p. 6. Other citations in my article "Fraternité". The material collected by Lécuyer (cf. note 13) shows that *fraternitas* was used in the 5th century only sporadically and then as a simple alternate of *collegium.*

Considering these facts one might be tempted to say that the rediscovery of the concept of collegiality by the theologians and the Church assembled in council is a great gain because in it the basic structure of the undivided Church of the patristic age has become visible. There is, however, the danger of stopping short at the already somewhat hardened structure of the 5th century, instead of going all the way so as to discover behind the closed and juridically fixed *collegium episcoporum,* the brother-relationship pervading the whole Church as its sustaining foundation. Collegiality can unfold its full pastoral fruitfulness only when it is related back to the fundamental reality of those who through "the First-born of the Father" became brothers.[18]

3. *Collegiality of the Bishops and Primacy of the Pope*

Before taking up the question of the pastoral fruitfulness of the doctrine of collegiality, we must first deal with another question which no doubt has come to the reader's mind, namely, does this conception of the structure of the Church not disregard for all practical purposes the Catholic doctrine of the primacy of the Roman bishop or, at least, largely empty it of its meaning? What function can the primacy have here? At Vatican II similar questions were the main reason for the vehement opposition to the doctrine of the collegiality of the episcopal office. As a result of the controversy over this objection, the problems inherent in collegiality, its connection with the brother-relationship of the whole Church and similar problems were not sufficiently considered. After all the theological work already done in the discussions of this question, our answer may be brief.

The doctrine of the collegiality of bishops will bring some

---

[18] The root of the brotherliness of the Christians in the First-Born who makes them brethren has been beautifully described by Gregory of Nyssa, following the thoughts of Origen (*e.g., De oratione* 15, 4 GCS 2 [Koetschau] 335) *Ref. conf. Eunomii* 80-3, ed. W. Jaeger III, pp. 345f. Extensive treatment in my article in "Fraternité" and the new edition of *Die christliche Bruederlichkeit.*

modifications, by no means unimportant, of certain presentations of the doctrine of the primacy, but it will not nullify it. Instead, it will point up its central theological significance. This may make it more understandable to our Orthodox brethren. The primacy cannot be patterned on the model of an absolute monarchy as if the pope were the unrestricted monarch of a centrally constituted, supernatural State called Church; but it means that within the network of the Churches communicating and thus forming the Church of God there is one official point, the *Sedes Romana,* by which the unity of faith and communion must be orientated.

This official center of the collegiality of bishops is not the result of a human need or purpose (although it might be suggested also by such reflections), but exists because the Lord himself established, beside and together with the office of "the twelve", also the special office of the Rock. To the eschatological sign of "the twelve" is added the sign of the Rock which is likewise taken from the eschatological symbolism of Israel. From these resulted, after the resurrection of Christ, the twofold office: the office of the witnesses and the office of the first witness in which St. Peter figures in the resurrection accounts and in the lists of the apostles.[19] Through the theology of St. Irenaeus (which, unfortunately, was later largely forgotten) this view became the theological conception the early Catholic Church had of itself.

---

[19] 1 Cor. 15, 5. The same tradition appears in Luke 24, 34 (to which Mark 16, 12 is related, also in Mark 16, 7. πρῶτος with which Matthew introduces Peter in his list of the apostles (10, 2-4) probably refers to the same tradition. Cf. Seeberg, *Wer war Petrus.* This has been reprinted together with two other contributions (Darmstadt, 1961). For the foundation of the idea of the rock in the symbolic language of Israel, cf. the instructive study by J. Jeremias, "Golgotha" (Leipzig, 1926). This work is extremely informative for a correct understanding of our Lord's commission to Simon Peter. Other pertinent and illuminating studies are: J. Ringer, "Das Felsenwort" in *Begegnung der Christen* (Festschrift O. Karrer, edited by Roesele-Cullmann, 1959), pp. 271-347; J. Betz, "Christus-petra-Petrus," in *Kirche und Ueberlieferung* (Festschrift, Geiselmann, edited by Betz-Fries, 1960), pp. 1-21.

This view contains the foundation of a fully consistent doctrine of the primacy, altogether consonant with its biblical origins.[20]

We cannot develop these thoughts more fully here. For our purposes it may be enough to state that the primacy of the bishop of Rome in its original meaning is not opposed to the collegial character of the Church but is a primacy of communion in the midst of the Church living as a community and understanding itself as such. It means, we repeat, the faculty and the right to decide authoritatively, within the network of communication, where the Word of the Lord is witnessed correctly, and consequently, where there is true communion. It presupposes the *communio ecclesiarum* and can be understood correctly only in reference to it.

II

THE PASTORAL IMPLICATIONS OF THE DOGMATIC STATEMENT

We come at last to the question of the pastoral implications of the doctrine of collegiality. We purposely say "implications", not practical application or some similar phrase. The pastoral concerns are not merely a pious gloss added to dogma, but dogma itself implies pastoral problems. In other words, the doctrine of the collegiality of the episcopal office and, with it, of the Church itself is not just a theory for specialists but a dogmatic statement and one immediately related to men and to the realities of life in the Church.

A fruitful pastoral theology of the future will have to overcome the sterile side-by-side system of mere theories and pragmatic recipes. It will have to find its way back to the original unity of the Bible and the Fathers. There the enunciated truths

[20] Cf. my expositions in Rahner-Ratzinger, *Episkopat und Primat* (1961), pp. 45-52 and my article "Kirche" in *Laepple-Schmaus, Wahrheit und Zeugnis* (1964), pp. 456-66.

are meant immediately and in their very substance for men. They are healing and saving truths in which pastoral concern and dogmatic truth are indissolubly intertwined. They are the truths of him who is equally "Logos" and "Shepherd".

Early Christian art understood this well when it represented the "Logos" as a shepherd, and saw in the shepherd the Eternal Word which is the true way for man.[21] We may perhaps consider this the first pastoral suggestion derived from the doctrine of collegiality, that is, dogmatic and pastoral theology cannot exist side by side but only in an intrinsic union.

Truth that is not ultimately concerned with man has no place in theology, and activity that ultimately does not come from truth revealed to us by Christ can hardly be called the care of souls. There are of course borderline areas in which these relations are somewhat distant and not quite apparent. Again, theory and practice will always remain different things, but their separation on principle is not compatible with the spirit of the Gospel. Let us try to put into focus some of the pastoral problems as they appear in light of the doctrine of collegiality.

1. *"I" and "We" in the Church*

One becomes a bishop, as we have seen, by entering into the community of bishops. In other words, the episcopal office exists essentially always in the plural, a "We", which gives significance to the individual "I". To enter upon a spiritual office, to which is entrusted the orderly function of the Church of God, means to fit oneself into a "We", which as a whole carries on the apostolic heritage. Community—being united with one another, having respect for one another, working with one another—these are essential to the structure of this office in the Church.

[21] Cf. V. Hamp, "Das Hirtenmotiv im Alten Testament," in *Festschrift für Kardinal Faulhaber* (1949), pp. 7-20; Th. K. Kempf, *Christus der Hirt, Ursprung und Deutung einer altchristlichen Symbolgestalt* (1942); J. Jeremias, ποιμήν, in ThWNT VI, pp. 484-98.

It seems to me that something very important emerges here, a situation of very general and far-reaching significance that enlightens the whole structure of Christian realities. Although the Christian faith has pointed up the importance of the individual who is called to eternal life, yet the "I" is in all things fitted into a more comprehensive "We" from which and for which it lives. We may perhaps say that this pluralistic structure of Christian life and the spiritual office in its ultimate depth is related to the mystery of the triune God in whom the eternal God, without injury to his indivisible unity and oneness, comprises the "We" of the Father, the Son and the Holy Spirit; a God who is one not in the formless unity of the rigid monad but in the plentiful reality of infinite love.

To describe this unity of the divine persons, patristic theology has coined the concept of *perichoresis* according to which this unity is an eternal dynamic interchange and interpenetration of Spirit and Spirit, of love and love.[22] Is this not a much more valid representation of the indivisible unity of the Church than the image of the divine majesty preferred by the court theology of the early Byzantine emperors, which was meant at the same time to be a justification of the Arian concept of God? [23] The unity of the Church is based on the *perichoresis* of the "Churches", on the *perichoresis* of the episcopal office, on the interpenetration of the manifold vitality of the dynamic "We", the dispenser of which is the office of the successors of the apostles as it is represented in the "We" of the episcopal college.

As the pluralistic structure of this office appears related to the fundamental mystery of the "We" of the three persons in the one God, so it is also related to the "We" of the whole Church and

[22] M. Schmaus, *Perichorese,* in LThK VIII, pp. 274ff.
[23] The contrast between the belief in the Trinity and the theology of divine monarchy demanded by political rulers is shown by E. Peterson, "Der Monotheismus als politisches Problem," in *Theologische Traktate* (1951), pp. 45-147.

is an image of its brotherliness. In other words, ultimately there is collegiality of the bishops when there is brotherliness of the Church; and the collegiality of the bishops fulfills its meaning only if it serves that brotherliness and if it is actualized in a brotherly spirit.

It seems to me that putting the declarations of Vatican II into ecclesiastical practice ushers in an important task. The proper appreciation of this will depend on whether or not the renewal of the doctrine of collegiality will result in a reform of the Church. For, against this doctrine, fears have already been voiced on the part of Protestants lest it lead to a yet greater clericalism in the Church and thus deepen the chasm between separated Christians. It is feared that the increased importance of the episcopacy may lead to a further lessening of the importance of the priesthood and especially of the laity in the Church.[24]

This danger will be effectively obviated only if the increased importance of the bishops is understood as giving increased importance to the Churches of God entrusted to them; if the individual bishop, enmeshed in the college of the bishops who are guiding the Church of God, in his turn knows himself obligated to a brotherly union with his presbyters and community. In other words, collegiality of the bishops fulfills its meaning only

[24] G. Maron, "Credo in Ecclesiam?" Reflections on the work of the Second Vatican Council, in *Materialdienst des konfessionskundlichen Instituts Bensheim* 15 (1964), pp. 1-8. Details, however, of this otherwise rewarding contribution are not exact enough to be convincing. The specter of an imminent *Credo in Ecclesiam* is quite unreal, apart from the fact that the formula appears in the ancient Symbols as the *Credo Ecclesiam* which is found in the Apostolic and Nicene creeds. The attempt to present the position of St. Jerome which after the separation of *ordo* and *jurisdictio* in the Middle Ages had become prevalent, as the authentic position of the ancient Church, and to see in the pastor the legitimate equivalent of the ancient *episcopus,* thus identifying the Protestant concept of office with that of the ancient Church and calling the constructions of Vatican II a dangerous innovation, is riddled with so many breaks and gaps that it cannot be considered an objective interpretation of the situation. Still the fears voiced here should make us cautious.

if the individual bishop really and truthfully represents his individual Church and thus, through him, a part of the Church's
plenitude is inserted into the totality of the Church's unity.

Thus, it will be an important obligation to insure that the increased importance of the episcopal office does not result in
making individual bishops little popes, as it were, by increasing
and strengthening their monarchical powers; rather, they must
be placed more clearly in the multiple relationship with their
brethren with whom they govern the Church of God. Against
this background the character of service and the ultimately pastoral meaning of the bishop's office will be seen. The bishop is
related on the one hand to his brethren in the same office, but
also to his brothers and sisters in the same grace who are, like
himself, baptized in the name of Jesus Christ. He can meet his
episcopal brethren in the right way only if he always comes to
them from the brotherly union of those who have the same faith.

Let us make these thoughts still more concrete. If this is the
situation, there can be no room for egotism in dioceses or communities that are concerned only with themselves, leaving all the
rest to the care of God and the Holy See. There must be a common responsibility one for another. Being catholic means, then,
being united with others;[25] to help one another in case of need;
to learn by that which is good in others and to share generously
one's own good; it means trying to become acquainted with one
another and accepting each other's differences. Of course mere
pious exhortations will not be sufficient. It will be an important
task of the future to develop practical ways of mutual communication, exchange and assistance. We shall return to this in
another connection.

Let us mention only one example here. The most human and
at the same time the most Christian interrelationship among
Christians and Christian communities, which is part of the

[25] Y. Congar, *Der Laie* (1956), especially pp. 542-49. (English ed.:
Lay People in the Church (1957), especially chap. IV).

doctrine of collegiality, is the hospitality of Christians. Jean Daniélou, who has written some of the most beautiful pages on this subject, describes the experiences of a Chinese friend of his who made a pilgrimage on foot from Peking to Rome. He noticed that hospitality grew less the closer he came to his goal. "In central Asia everything went well; as he passed through the Slavic countries the situation was tolerable; but when he reached the Latin countries there was no hospitality at all." [26]

Thanks be to God, we have had different experiences. From the hospitality practiced at the Eucharistic Congress in Munich in 1960, Christians have been united in bonds that will last many years. But should not such things be possible apart from official occasions? Should not such mutual interest be shown in the sphere of simple humanity and Christian spirit, apart from all organization? Where there is no spontaneity of real life, the efficiency of organizers is to no avail.

2. *The Mystical and Eucharistic Body of Christ*

From about the 12th century on, a distinction is made in the episcopal office between the *ordo* and *jurisdictio, i.e.,* between the power of ordination and the power of governing. The power of ordination is, then, particularly related to the "true Body of Christ" in the holy eucharist in which the priest, by virtue of the *ordo,* consecrates the bread in holy mass, while the power of jurisdiction is said to be related to "the Mystical Body of Christ".[27]

[26] J. Daniélou, *Vom Geheimnis der Geschichte* (1955), p. 77. The same chapter "Deportation und Gastfreundschaft" has many suggestions on this point.

[27] K. Mörsdorf has recently sought to clarify the relationship between *ordo* and *jurisdictio* (Weihe- und Hirtengewalt), *e.g.,* "Weihegewalt und Hirtengewalt in Abgrenzung und Bezug," in *Misc. Comillas* 16 (1951), pp. 95-110; *Die Entwicklung der Zweigliedrigkeit der Hierarchie,* in MThZ 3 (1952), pp. 1-16; important indications also by L. Hoedl, *Die Geschichte der scholastischen Literatur und der Theologie der Schluesselgewalt I* (1960); *idem., De jurisdictione: Ein unveroeffentlichter Traktat des Herveus Natalis. . . . ueber die Kirchengewalt* (1959); *idem.,* J. Quidort von Paris, *De confessionibus audiendis* (1962).

It should be noted that because of this view medieval theology denied that episcopal consecration was a separate degree of the sacrament of holy orders, since in the ordination of the priest the full power of eucharistic consecration was conferred, to which nothing could be added.[28] Today, in the light of biblical and patristic studies, we consider this distinction, if not insignificant, at least insufficient. Mentioned several times in our discussion of collegiality, its clarification from this point of view entails far-reaching consequences.

If the above distinction were to be accepted without reservations the following argument would be possible: the power of ordination refers only to sacramental action, especially the holy eucharist. This has nothing to do with collegiality since the *actio liturgica* of the priest in holy mass is here and now the priest's alone. The power of jurisdiction refers indeed to the Church, but only the pope has jurisdiction over the whole Church while the bishop has jurisdiction over a limited part in which he (except for the pope) is alone competent. Hence, jurisdiction also cannot be taken in a collegial sense. The ultimate conclusion would be that collegiality has nothing at all to do with the essential functions of the episcopal office, but may be regarded at most as a moral postulate in the accidental relations of the bishops among themselves.

If anywhere at all, then, it becomes evident here that the schematic thought of scholastic argumentation (the importance of which remains undeniable) breaks down in dealing with the many-sided realities of the Church. We find this already and most of all in this treatment of the holy eucharist. For the eucharist is not at all that individualistic act of consecration which the priest performs himself alone by virtue of an *accidens physicum, i.e.,* of the sacramental character, without relation to others and to the Church. The eucharist is by its very essence

[28] Cf. J. Lechner, *Die Sakramentenlehre des Richard von Mediavilla* (1925). See the texts in Thomas Aquinas, IV *Sent.* d. 24 q. 3 a. 2 quaestiunc. 2 ad 2; *Bonaventura* IV *Sent.* d. 24 p. 2 a. 2 q. 3, etc.

sacramentum ecclesiae. There is an inseparable connection between the eucharistic and the Mystical Body of the Lord. We cannot think of one without the other.

From among the many texts that could be cited, we quote only the words of William of St. Thierry which express so fully the mind of St. Augustine: "Eating the Body of Christ is nothing else but becoming the Body of Christ." [29] "Collegiality" is present in "sacramentality"; the holy eucharist is by its very essence the sacrament of Christian fraternity, of mutual union through union with Christ. Accordingly, in the ancient Church, nearly all words signifying the holy eucharist are names for the church itself; *koinonía, symphonía, eirênê, agape, pax, communio*— all these expressions without distinction signify the indivisible mystery of eucharist and Church all in one.[30]

St. Thomas Aquinas, as the heir of St. Augustine's tradition, who in turn was but the interpreter of the heritage of the ancient Church, calls the *res sacramenti* of the eucharist, the reality it communicates and means, the unity of the Mystical Body of Christ.[31] It may well be said that the separation of the doctrine of the eucharist and ecclesiology, which can be noted from the 11th and 12th centuries onward, represents one of the most unfortunate pages of medieval theology (meritorious in so many other questions) because both thereby lost their center. A doctrine of the eucharist that is not related to the community of the Church misses its essence as does an ecclesiology that is not conceived with the eucharist as its center.

It would seem then that the thesis that the *ordo* is related only

---

[29] PL. 184, 403. A large number of texts of this kind and thorough analysis of the whole development is to be found in H. de Lubac, *Corpus Mysticum. L'eucharistie et l'église au moyen age* (1949 [2]). Cf. also Ratzinger, *Volk und Haus Gottes in Augustins Lehre von der Kirche* (1954), especially pp. 188-218.

[30] Cf. L. Hertling's work mentioned in note 9; also Guyot's work mentioned there.

[31] *Sum. Theol.* III q. 73 a. 3c: . . . res sacramenti est unitas corporis mystici . . . Cf. *ibid.* ad 3: . . . sicut baptismus dicitur sacramentum fidei . . . ita Eucharistia dicitur sacramentum caritatis.

to the *corpus eucharisticum* and has nothing to do with "collegiality" will have to be turned around so as to read: if and because the *ordo* is related to the eucharist its whole function is related to *koinonía* which is the contents of the eucharist and the original concept of "collegiality" in one. This can be proved even by the very usage of the terms inasmuch as the word *ordo* originally was an alternate for *collegium.* In pagan Rome the word *ordo* designated the estates of classes of the people where the *ordo amplissimus* of the senate was placed over against the *populus Romanus; ordo et plebs, ordo et populus* are current expressions where *ordo* signifies those who govern the city.[32]

In the formula *nos et plebs tua sancta* of the canon of the Roman mass we have an echo of this conception in the spirit of which was also coined the expression *ordo episcoporum* which declares that the bishops are an estate, a community, a *collegium.* The very idea of sacrament contains the idea of community. The sacrament is not a physical entity to which is ordered a separate power of jurisdiction; it is itself the builder of a new community and is meant to serve this community.

This is seen very plainly in the structure of the eucharistic liturgy. Its subject is the "We" of the holy People of God and its intrinsic place is the community of the saints that already shines through the *Confiteor* and is clearly put before the soul in the account of the institution. The remembrance of the sublime multitude of the saints of the whole Church and especially of the local Church of Rome, conjured up in the *Communicantes* and in the *Nobis quoque;* the recall of Abel, Melchisedech, Abraham, these great Old Testament types of Christ's sacrifice in the *Supra quae;* the remembrance of the living and dead of the community in the two *Memento* prayers; finally, mentioning the local bishop and the common bishop of the Apostolic See in Rome as well as all the faithful participants of the Christian cult in the

---

[32] See the expositions by M. Guy in Guyot, *loc. cit.* footnote 9, p. 93. Cf. also the texts and citations under the title *ordo* in A. Blaise-H. Chirat, *Dict. latin-français des auteurs chrétiens* (1954), p. 584.

very first prayer of the canon—all these are not mere ornaments but the intrinsically necessary expression of the *koinonia* of the eucharistic action.

Mention of the bishop of Rome is here the representative-comprehensive expression for inserting the eucharistic celebration into the totality of the *communio ecclesiarum* by which alone the local eucharistic celebration is certified as true participation of the indivisible Body of Christ which the Church receives as a community. This mention is, therefore, not only an expression of the primacy of the bishop of Rome but of the unity of the communion-community in him and represents at the same time the collegiality of the bishops and the fraternity of all the Churches.

This opens up another wide horizon of pastoral insights. Not only is the rigid opposition of *ordo* and *jurisdictio* dissolved and the intrinsic union of the two made clear, thus resulting in an entirely different conception and practice of the two, but, in general, there is made possible a new and fundamental understanding of the sacramental reality, the attitude of prayer as well as of that which is commonly called "government" in the Church.

Here are great problems for the theology and pastoral care of the future. These can be merely mentioned, not developed, within the limits of this article. We conclude the foregoing reflections with this summary: by freeing the concept of collegiality from the rigid opposition of *ordo* and *jurisdictio,* and by showing its root in the sacramental reality of the Church, the contrasting alternative of either mere juridical or mere moral understanding is dissolved, and there appears its peculiarly Christian form of a true and obligatory community fashioned entirely from its sacramental reality. The background of the sacramentally founded brotherliness of Christians is especially pointed up. The collegiality of the bishops is only a segment of this which must not be isolated.[33]

[33] This point was stressed especially by H. Küng at the Konstanz conversations. Cf. also his expositions in *Strukturem der Kirche* (1962).

3. *Unity in Plurality*

"Collegiality" applies not only to the episcopal office but to the structure of the whole Church. It means that the one Church is built up through the communion of the many Churches and that, consequently, unity of the Church essentially comprises the element of plurality and plenitude. This has always been known as a principle but has not always been sufficiently respected in practice. A Protestant theologian in Germany some years ago coined the formula: the unitary Church prevents the unity of the Church.[34] Though this statement is extreme, it cannot be denied all justification. The unity of the spirit can be preserved only where there remains room for many charisms.

The implications of this truth extend over a wide area beginning with the structure of the whole Church down to the daily life of individual parishes. As far as the structure of the whole Church is concerned, it has become plainly improper to deduce this truth from some political model. The all-too-ready attempts to establish a basis for the primacy with arguments drawn from the philosophy of Plato and Aristotle, which declares the monarchy as the best form of government,[35] are just as much doomed to failure as the attempt to describe the Church by the incommensurate category of the monarchy. The relations of sacrament and order, of the Petrine and episcopal offices, of the collegiality of the bishops and the fraternity of Christians, of the plurality

[34] H. Dombois in *Begegnung der Christen* (Karrer-Festschrift, see note 9), p. 395: "Church unity and unitary Church are according to experience in history so contradictory that the type of the unitary Church cannot be the type of Church unity." Cf. also H. Dombois, "Zur Revision des Kirchengeschichtsbildes," in *Die Katholizitaet der Kirche,* edited by Staehlin-Asmussen (1957).

[35] Such is the argumentation of Robert Bellarmine's *Controversiae* II, 1, pp. 1ff. The sequence of the chapter headings is: (1) What is the best form of government? (2) Proof of the first thesis: simple monarchy is preferable to simple aristocracy and democracy. . . . (4) Prescinding from all circumstances, pure monarchy is to be preferred without qualifications.

of the Churches and the unity of the Church, which we recognize as original realities, exceed all categories of political philosophy by such a degree that no model taken from them could do justice to our subject.

But, as mentioned above, the element of plurality in unity is not a matter of general principles only. It reaches down into the organism of the individual parish which, on the one hand, has its monarchic summit in the pastor and yet must not turn into a monarchy of the pastor but must leave room for advice from the laity and his clerical brethren, especially for different temperaments and their manifestations which have a right to exist. There should be in the Church, more definitely perhaps than is commonly the case, a form of toleration that would refrain from forcing particular forms on everyone, leaving no room for possible ways of piety. Not everything is suitable for everyone nor are all created in exactly the same pattern.

These reflections applied to the whole Church would mean that there should also be initiatives from the various parts of the Church; initiatives that indeed would have to be coordinated, clarified and supervised by the center, but should not simply be substituted by uniform directions. Why is it that today there are no such things as the letters of St. Ignatius of Antioch, of St. Polycarp, of St. Dionysius of Corinth? Why should it not be possible that bishops' conferences address themselves to each other in words of thanks or encouragement or even correction of false ways if such have been followed?

Let us dwell for a moment on the bishops' conferences that seem to offer themselves today as the best means of concrete plurality in unity. They have their prototype in the synodal activity[36] of the regionally different "colleges" of the ancient Church.[37] They are also a legitimate form of the collegiate structure of the Church. One not infrequently hears the opinion that

[36] See the work of W. de Vries mentioned in note 8.
[37] The material collected by Lécuyer (see note 13) proves that there

the bishops' conferences lack all theological basis and could therefore not act in a way that would oblige the individual bishop. The concept of collegiality, so it is said, could be applied only to the common action of the entire episcopate. Here again we have a case where a one-sided and unhistorical systematization breaks down.

The *suprema potestas in universam ecclesiam* which canon 228, 1 ascribes to the ecumenical council applies, of course, only to the college of bishops as a whole in union with the bishop of Rome. But is it always a question of the *suprema potestas* in the Church? Would this not be quite outrageously reminiscent of the disciples' quarrel about their rank?

We should rather say that the concept of collegiality, besides the office of unity which pertains to the pope, signifies an element of variety and adaptability that basically belongs to the structure of the Church, but may be actuated in many different ways. The collegiality of bishops signifies that there should be in the Church (under and in the unity guaranteed by the primacy) an ordered plurality. The bishops' conferences are, then, one of the possible forms of collegiality that is here partially realized but with a view to the totality.[38]

After what has been said it appears important that the bishops' conferences do not exist side by side but in a kind of *perichoresis,* lest the movement toward plurality lead to splintering. Mutual

---

was still in the 5th century, besides the universal use of the concept of *collegium,* a frequent particular use of it. I cite only two of the texts presented by Lécuyer: Caelestinus I, *Ep.* 4 PL 50, 435c-436a: "Massiliensis vero Ecclesiae sacerdotum . . . et vestro eum audiendum collegio delegamus." Felix II, *Ep.* 3, 2, ed. E. Schwartz, *Publizistische Sammlungen zum Accacianischen Schisma* (Munich, 1934), p. 75, lin. 23-25: "Ad quam rem de collegio nostro fratres et coepiscopos nostros Vitalem et Misenum . . . ordinatione direximus." Lécuyer is of the opinion that *collegium nostrum* means the Roman synod.

[38] Cf. the important expositions by J. Hamer, "Les conférences épiscopales exercice de la collégialité," in *Nouv. Rev Theol.* 95 (1963), pp. 966-69.

exchange will be more important the more the individual areas of the Church unfold their particular characteristics. In comparison to the tasks of former times, the primacy will face quite new tasks in aiding and initiating such exchanges.

4. *Renewal from Origins—toward Hope*

The movement in the Church that seeks to reactivate the principle of collegiality in its structure may be regarded both as a leap forward and a return to origins and beginnings. These two are in the last analysis not contradictory but significant for the way in which the Church exists in and between the times. On the one hand, it is based entirely on a fact of the past, namely, the life, death and resurrection of Jesus Christ which the Church proclaims on the basis of the witness of the apostles as the salvation of men and the source of eternal life. The revelation of God on which the Church lives occurred in a definite historical *here* and *now* and thus the Church is inevitably connected with those singular historical events.

The obligatory norm of renewal can only come about by a new orientation from its origin. The Church cannot be manipulated at will. The Church cannot become up-to-date according to the wishes of the times; Christ and his Church cannot be accommodated to the times and their fashions; it is the different times that must be measured by the norm of Christ. Here lies the difference between genuine and false reformation and renewal which, at first sight, may look so much alike that they are apt to be confused.

True renewal of the Church will always consist only in cutting off excrescences of certain times (which will ever and again grow up unnoticed) so that the pure image of its original reality may shine forth. Mere concessions to the times or mere "modernization" are always false renewal which at first arouses enthusiasm but is soon seen as the delusive hope it is, for in the competition for modernization the Church will never come up first. In the course of history the well-intentioned modernizations have always proved very soon to be obstacles which tied the Church to a definite epoch and had a paralyzing effect on the power of its message.

Although the renewal of the Church can come only from turning to its origin, it must be something altogether different from restoration, the romantic glorification of the past, which would be just as unchristian as mere modernization. This is so because the historical Jesus on whom the Church is based is at the same time the coming Christ in whom the Church hopes; because Christ is not only the Christ of yesterday but also the Christ of today and forever (cf. Heb. 13,8).

As the faith of the Old Testament has a twofold orientation in terms of time: one toward the past, namely, the miracle of the Red Sea by which Israel was saved from the Egyptians and which was the founding of its existence as the People of God; and one forward, toward the days of the Messiah, in which the promises made to Abraham would be fulfilled; so the historical existence of the Church has two poles: it is referred back to its founding in the death and resurrection of the Lord, and forward to his Second Coming when he will fulfill his promise of making of the world a new heaven and a new earth.

Thus, the Church, while, and exactly because, it is based on the past, is turned toward the things that are to come "in hope". The basic attitude of the Christian is not marked by restoration but by hope. In its effort for renewal the Church sheds the entanglements of history not in order to restore an ideal state of the past but to move toward the Lord, to be free for his new call. In turning to him the Church moves into the future knowing full well that the ultimate future can be no other than Christ.

It would not be difficult to illustrate these truths by the theme of collegiality whose renewed emphasis, on the one hand, marks a return to the origins, and, on the other, cannot be a reconstruction or restoration of particular historical forms, but an opening toward the future in which the original realities are to become effective in a new way. Without going into further detail we wish only to state in general that the most important task after Vatican II will be to create again in Christians this attitude of hope which is essential to Christian faith, and to orientate them exclusively toward the Lord who is our beginning and our future.

EDWARD SCHILLEBEECKX, O.P.

Born in Antwerp, Belgium, November 12, 1914.
He became a Dominican in 1934, and was ordained in 1941. He pursued his studies at Le
Saulchoir in Etiolles, France and at the Sorbonne
in Paris, becoming a master and doctor of theology.
From 1943 to 1957 he taught at the Dominican
Studium in Louvain, Belgium, and has been, since
1958, professor of dogmatic theology at the Uni-
versity of Nijmegen, Holland. He is an advisor to
the Dutch episcopacy at Vatican Council II.
Among his many publications are: *The Sacra-
mental Economy of Salvation* (1952); *Mary,
Mother of the Redemption* (1964); *Christ, the
Sacrament of the Encounter with God* (1963);
Huwelijk, aardse werkelijkheid en heilsmysterie,
Vol. I (1964).

Edward Schillebeeckx, O.P./*Nijmegen, Netherlands*

The Church and Mankind

THE PROBLEM

In our age we have become aware, more than in the past, that our salvation comes about within the one reality that is ours, within the scope of our own life in this world. Everywhere there is evidence of a reaction against any kind of religious practice which is alien to this world. Christianity had come to be regarded as something added on to life here on earth with its sorrow and joy, its fear and hope, its activities and moments of recollection. Many Christians used to practice their Christianity as a superstructure erected on top of their normal lives. Frequently they would look upon this life as merely matter, without religious significance in itself, for the occasional exercise of Christian virtues. Life's own significance had, in their eyes, nothing to do with Christianity.

Real religion, they held, was only practiced within a church edifice or by saying a few prayers at home—in other words, at the periphery of life. As a result, many Christians gave the impression that Christianity was an ideological superstructure, or a special department where people talked about forgiveness, redemption, the cross and resurrection, while life in this world waited outside. The human problems of life on this earth failed to get from them the attention they received from non-believers to the benefit of mankind.

At present, there is a strong emerging realization that adherence to faith is not a mere structure superimposed upon human and secular relationships, which would in fact be what they are, with or without Christianity, and so would be unaffected by faith. Consequently, reaction against ghetto-Catholicism and ghetto-Christianity is characteristic of present-day religious awareness among both Catholics and Reformed Christians. Service to a world which is growing into a closer unity; the ethical commitment imposed upon Western man by the advanced position which the West enjoys in contrast to the rest of the world, particularly the underdeveloped countries; the plans for a dynamic blueprint to set up a society upon earth that shall be worthy of men—all this is seen, also by the religious man of today, as the concrete, even the principal way in which he purposes to give form to his religion and to Christianity.

Hand in hand with this new religious awareness there is opposition to an exotic religious vocabulary. Religious ideas have to be couched in "profane" words, in language that springs from the profound realities of human existence. People want their Christianity to be less explicit and prefer it to work implicitly, almost incognito, toward salvation within their secular human relationships.

This current phenomenon, however, has one drawback. Many believers are at a loss as to what to do about the Church as an objective reality. Sociological researches draw attention to the fact that some kind of faith in God as the basis of all existence, and faith, too, in the Man Jesus, who by his life has shown the meaning of God's love for men, actually exist in persons who had "practiced" earlier in their lives but do not belong at present to any Church: they also show that precisely these persons no longer find any room in their belief for the "Church".

They could only accept the Church—and with enthusiasm— if Church meant no more than the establishment of a community among men, the real expression of the community that human fellowship ought to build up in the world. There is talk of "Christianity without a Church", a Christianity in which fellowship and brotherhood appear as the essence of Church.

The lines of our essay take two directions. We inquire first into the increasingly "ecclesial" tendency in the world, or rather in mankind; and secondly, we inquire into the tendency within the Church to sanctify the secular. On the one hand, the human fellowship in Christ is surely the heart of the Church as a phenomenon: St. Thomas calls sanctifying grace *gratia fraterna,* the grace that establishes brotherhood. On the other hand, as believers, we cannot help admitting that the Church is a community *sui juris,* or rather, *juris Christi.* But *ipso facto* we then create a certain distance between the Church and mankind. There are boundaries between the Church and humanity, and yet they are fluid, not hard and fast. Into the implications of this we now propose to inquire, for the sake of a mankind that grows away from the Church and for the sake of faith in the Church as founded by Christ.

I

THE UNITY OF MANKIND AND THE COMMUNION OF SAINTS

Mankind's specific unity from an anthropological viewpoint must formally (*formaliter*) be based, not on its biological substratum, but, by its very nature, on a community of *persons,* a *communio.* It can only be built on a value-appeal, the community-building force of truly human values. This means simply that human unity has its origin in oneness of vocation and destiny.

Communio among all men is the immanent human expression of this single vocation. Human unity in its essence is not a mere datum: it is a task to be carried out. This task, we know from revelation, is in fact the response to a free and gracious act of God. The *koinonía* or community which he wills is also his gift. By his absolute self-communication to men he at once reveals himself as their highest value and reveals mankind to itself as his People, the People of God. By the granting of his grace God constitutes mankind "the People of God". Communion among men is the reflection, immanent in mankind's history, of man's transcending communion with the living God: the God-willed unity of mankind is therefore nothing less than the *communio Sanctorum,* the community of mankind sanctified.

Not only is the fact of this community an undue gift to men, but the manner of producing it also has its origin in a sovereign, free act of God. The history of salvation in both the Old and the New Testaments, even though the outlook of the ancient Near Eastern peoples plays its role in them, makes this fact clear: God did not intend "abstract" fundamental values to be the basis on which human unity was to be realized. He intends to gather all men into a holy community of persons on the basis of values that were expressed in living persons as in prototypes.

Time and again someone is chosen from among ourselves to be the means of salvation in forming the "great gathering" of men from the diaspora, the People of God.[1] The manner, not due to men, in which God establishes a community among them is that of representative or vicarious mediation: for the sake of one man, whom God freely calls for the purpose, salvation—or destruction —is brought to many. In the Old and the New Testaments, time and again, the representative function whether of one man or of a limited collectivity is essential for salvation or destruction:

[1] See J. Scharbert, *Heilsmittler im Alten Testament und im Alten Orient,* (*Quaest. Disp.* 23, 24, Freiburg im Br., 1964).

Adam, Noah, Moses, the twelve Patriarchs, "Israel", the "King", the Servant of Yahweh, Jesus.

In the Bible the establishment of a community through mediation implies that election and universal mission coalesce into one. Thus, however gradually and hesitantly, Israel did at last become aware of her election to be an example to all peoples—of her election for the service of all men. In the Old Testament conception it is to Yahweh's redemptive covenant with Noah after the Flood that the totality of mankind throughout history owes its existence. And in connection with that covenant a catalogue is drawn up of all the nations existing in the world as conceived by the ancients (Gen. 10).[2] Again, in Abraham "shall all nations be blessed" (Gen. 12, 3; 18, 18; 22, 18). His election, too, is God's ratification of universal salvation.

The notion of mediatorship shows us that men are dependent upon one another and that God in bringing his transcendent salvation means to preserve the structure of human fellowship. Through men he wants to bring salvation to men. The notions of "the first-born among many brethren" (Rom. 8, 29), which embraces prototypical religious fellowship, and of "God's first-born son" (Ex. 4, 22), in which divine choice and service to the neighbor are united, are led up to throughout the Old Testament. They suggest the fundamental notion that salvation is a gift conveyed through man's fraternal service to others according to God's election. Even Israel, the People of God, is, when chosen, "God's first-born son" (*loc. cit.*): Israel is personified, initially, in the vicarious figure of the King, who is therefore eponymously called "Son of God" (*e.g.,* 2 Sam. 7, 14; Ps. 2, 7), and ultimately in the figure of the coming Messiah and Son of Man, "the Son of God" *par excellence.*

Jesus is not merely one of us—he represents "Israel, the Son

[2] See G. von Rad, "Das z. erste Buch Mose" in *Das Alte Testament Deutsch,* 2 (Göttingen, 1949), pp. 119ff.

of God", but in an incomparably deeper sense: in a uniquely transcendent manner he is "the Son of the Father". Nevertheless, he is our fellowman "taken from among men" (Heb. 5, 1), "born of a woman" (Gal. 4, 4). Election and fraternal service, "Son of God", servant of God and men—these ideas find their highest fulfillment in Jesus. And so it is in him that the "great gathering" of all men around God, *he ekklesia toû Theoû* (1 Cor. 11, 22; 15, 9) is formed into a mutual *communio* of men with Christ as their center—a "Church of Christ", *hai ekklesiai toû Christoû* (Rom. 16, 16). Scattered mankind becomes in Christ unified mankind (Eph. 2, 15) founded on the "eschatological Man",[3] the *eschatos Adam* (1 Cor. 15, 45). He is a vivifying Spirit (*loc. cit.*), not merely man, but a man who "gives life" to his fellow-men.

Mankind, then, has received salvation through the fraternal service of one chosen from among ourselves—Jesus Christ, the Elect of God, the Son of the Father. This fact of Christ, which took place in our history and in our secular and human affairs, has had a real effect on human history. Mankind's new fundamental but real unity and new structure as a community rests upon God's universal saving will. This will is not an actuality that is simply beyond history; it has manifested itself visibly within history in the "objective redemption", that is, in the personal life of Jesus, representative man, Son of God, appearing among us in our history.

In one Man—the *homo principalis,* as Irenaeus says,[4] *i.e.,* he who stands at the wellspring of the new mankind, which *ipso facto* he has gathered into a community—in this one Man all

---

[3] See among others E. Peterson, "Die Kirche," *Theologische Traktate* (Munich, 1951), pp. 409-28.

[4] Irenaeus, *Adv. Haereses* V.21.1 (*PG* 7.1179). *Principalis* (*archaios*) in *Adv. Haer.* means "standing at the point of," and is used in connection with Irenaeus' theory of Recapitulation. Christ stands at the new beginning of all things.

men have already ascended through the passion to the glory with the Father.

Thus the history of Israel, which is a component of, and imbedded in, human history, takes on a new meaning. For human history, wherever it is made, has in this manner found grace with the Father and is already conclusively accepted by the Father in the *Eschaton,* Jesus Christ. For the Father has established Jesus who humbled himself, as the glorified Christ, the "Son of God in power" (Rom. 1, 4) at his own right hand. Consequently Christ is at once the Alpha and Omega of human history in its entirety (Apoc. 1, 8; 21, 6; 22, 13). As such, he is the key to history, not only in an exclusively transcendent manner beyond time and space, but his humanity now glorified is a truly historical humanity that has reached its consummation at a real point in history. In Jesus, history is finally and conclusively perfected with that kind of perfect achievement that persists in eternity. As representative, first of Israel, and so of mankind, he is the prototypical moment of mankind's history; this moment has already been inserted in eternal glory. And so our Lord, although in a dimension that exceeds our experience, gives our human history its final immanent meaning. Every historical human event wherever occurring, even in areas called "profane", can thus be understood only through the eschatological Man, Jesus Christ.

II

DIALECTICAL TENSION BETWEEN "MANKIND" AND THE CHURCH

Christ has bestowed a new religious meaning upon mankind in principle and in the concrete (*i.e.,* integrated in our own history). Nevertheless, between mankind "gathered" into a collectivity in principle and its actual manifestation in Christ there exists a certain distance. This distance and tension are embodied in Christ's Church. For it is in the Church, by free assent to the grace of justification, by acceptance of God's Word in faith, and by admission to baptism in the name of the Holy Trinity, that mankind's new religious meaning takes on the form that establishes an historical, visible, concrete community. When a man is incorporated into the Church, Christ's triumphant grace becomes a plain, historical, recognizable fact.[5] The result is that, at least from the ascension until the Second Coming, there is a certain distinction and dialectical tension between humanity redeemed in principle, at its source, and the Church.

In a series of articles of progressive subtlety, A. Vögtle, a Catholic biblical exegete, has demonstrated that Jesus, at least in his public teaching, nowhere manifests an intention of selecting from Israel a specific group of persons in order to form them into a separate community.[6] By his public preaching of God's dominion and by his call to repentance he plainly intended to gather not a remnant only but all of Israel and make of it the new Israel, the eschatological People of *God*. Sectarianism was alien to him. Radically he pursues the path of the history of salvation as Paul will afterward copy it: salvation is announced first to Israel, and then, according to the divine design, *via* Israel to the whole world.

Jesus' call of "the twelve" from among the group of disciples

---

[5] See among others K. Rahner, "Kirche und Parusie Christi," in *Catholica* 17 (1963), pp. 113-28.

[6] A. Vögtle, *Das öffentliche Wirken Jesu auf dem Hintergrund der Qumranbewegung* (Freiburger Universitätsreden, N.F., 27, Freiburg im Br., 1958, pp. 5-20, esp. pp. 15ff.); "Ekklesiologische Auftragsworte des Auferstandenen," in *Actes du Congrès internationale catholique des sciences bibliques à Bruxelles* (1959), pp. 892-906; "Jesus und die Kirche," in *Begenung der Christen,* ed. Hoesle-Cullman (Frankfurt am Main, 1960), pp. 54, 82; "Der Einzelne und die Gemeinschaft in der Stufenfolge der Christusoffenbarung," in *Sentire Ecclesiam,* ed. Daniélou and Vorgrimler, (Freiburg im Br., 1961), pp. 50-91; see also "Die Adam-Christus Typologie und der Menschensohn," in *Trierer Theol. Zeitschrift* (1951), pp. 209-28. See also footnote 7 below.

is clearly explained as a parable in action that his contemporaries could not mistake:[7] in "the twelve", the twelve Patriarchs of Israel are represented—a further proof of Jesus' purpose to win all Israel for the kingdom of heaven. Actually, however, all Israel does not adhere to his doctrine, but on the contrary, opposition to his activities grows ever stronger. Chiefly because of the massive dimensions the opposition assumed and as he sees the historical event of his death approaching and the violent form it is to take, Jesus begins within the limited circle of the disciples to interpret its meaning and to explain it in the light of the prophecy in Deutero-Isaiah: his death is to be an expiation "for the many" —that is, for all—and God has arranged it so beforehand. Not before his death and resurrection,[8] and only in connection with them, is he to speak to his disciples of "the Church which he is going to build upon the Rock" (Peter) (Matt. 16, 18f.; see John 21, 15-17).

This implies that the redeemed People of God will become after Jesus' death and resurrection an *Ecclesia Christi*—an historical, visible gathering or congregation of men around Christ, in visible communion with the "Rock" and the twelve apostles. This situation gives Jesus' community a special ecclesiastico-social structure, which as such does not coincide with the social structure of secular society.

We see, then, that on the one hand, in his public preaching Jesus never speaks of a Church with forms of organization, and that he lays down obedient acceptance of his message of salvation, here and now, in the *kairos* of the present moment, as the

[7] See A. Vögtle, *Das öffentliche Wirken Jesu,* p. 15; F. Braun, *Neues Licht auf die Kirche* (Einsiedeln, 1946), p. 71; A. Fridrichsen, "Messias und Kirche," in *Ein Buch von der Kirche* (Göttingen, 1951), p. 33; see K. Rengstorf, *Theol. Wörterb. z. N.T.* (Teil 2), pp. 321-28, s.v. *dodeka.*

[8] See A. Vögtle, "Messiasbekenntnis und Petrusverheissung," in *Biblische Zeitschrift,* N.F. 1 (1957), pp. 257-72 and 2 (1958), pp. 85-103. The connection between Peter's confession at Caesarea and Christ's promise of the *Ecclesia* is called secondary, *i.e.,* it is an "arrangement" of Matthew or of the Matthew tradition.

sole condition for entering the kingdom of God. And on the other hand, it is in the light of his death as an expiation for all men that he speaks of the founding of his Church. This he presents as a post-paschal event: "I *shall* build my Church." Holy Scripture, then, clearly connects the messianic suffering—Jesus' "going away"—with the post-paschal realization of the Church.

The Church is God's People with a special qualification: the People of God who through Jesus' death and resurrection become through the Spirit the Body of Christ—*soma Christoû*—the Body of the *Lord*. On earth this Body is built as "the Church" upon Peter, the Rock. The return to the Father—the vertical theme of Jesus' public preaching—becomes in the light of his death, explained to his apostles as reconciliation, after Easter and Pentecost also a horizontal theme: the building of a mutual community around the Rock. It becomes, consequently, a clear theme of a mankind redeemed with the purpose of an ecclesial brotherhood, a communal Church with its own initiation, its own cult, especially the sharing of the eucharistic table, a community guided and accompanied by a ministering office. Thus the death and glorification of Jesus, the Christ, have made access to this brotherhood, the sacramentally and historically visible Church, a condition for entrance into the kingdom of God.[9] The *communio* of believers gathered about its bishop (in communion with the Rock)—this *is* salvation, the Church of Christ. Precisely in this *koinonía* must the Father's absolute self-communication through the Son in the Holy Spirit find that historically visible realization, which is in truth the sign of all mankind's vocation. Hence the Church is not just a *koinonía,* a communion or sharing of grace with Christ, the fruit of his redemptive work, but it is also an institution for salvation to which the keys that make entrance possible into the kingdom of God have been entrusted. In contrast to Jesus' "Woe unto you, scribes and Pharisees", who bar

[9] Mark 10, 40 and Matthew 20, 20-23; Mark 14, 25; see Luke 22, 16. 18.

the entrance to the kingdom (Matt. 23, 13), Christ gives Peter the keys that open the gates.

III

THE BASIS OF THE DIALECTICAL TENSION

There is, then, a distance or interval between mankind, fundamentally and historically redeemed, and the community of Jesus built upon the Rock, which is the Church or body of "practicing Christians". To understand this distance we must first remember the connection laid by Holy Scripture between the messianic death—Jesus' "going away"—and the Church, which is only post-paschal and therefore a new reality, new even in comparison with that universal reality which is the People of God.

From our point of view the death of Jesus is mankind's rejection of him: Israel's rejection through its representative, the Sanhedrin; the Gentiles' rejection of him in the person of Pilate, and even the rejection by the hierarchy of the future Church in the persons of the apostles who ran away, and of Peter, who denied him. In his death Jesus stands alone, crushed by "the sins of the world"; alone in his surrender to the Father for the service of his fellowmen. That which achieved this reconciliation was, therefore, also the cause of Jesus' factual absence—the absence, in other words, of the source of grace. From our point of view, the breach of the covenant of grace was made complete by his death: mankind has banished from the world "the coming of God's kingdom" in Christ and so has expelled it from the *communio* of men.

Every death, of course, means bodily absence and the breaking off of relations with the dead as fellowmen. In the case of Jesus, however, it is a matter of the death of the only one who could bring redemption. From our point of view, this removal of Christ, the Man of grace, is therefore irrevocable. For the renewal of his relations with us through the resurrection is certainly not owing to us, not even to Christ's humanity as such. Only by understanding the profound importance of his death can we fully appreciate the basic saving significance of his resurrection, which, on account of the sacrifice that had been offered, made possible the sending of the Holy Spirit and the building of the Church. In the resurrection, which was a grace of the Father, the redemptive work of Jesus triumphed. But this triumph implies that henceforth our salvation depends upon someone who is absent from our experience, Jesus Christ.

We may justly conclude from this that the final state of our condition as it was created by original sin is "a situation in which the *privation* of supernatural grace can *only be removed sacramentally,* a situation in which man found himself ever since, and, because of the breach of the covenant with God, was made complete through man's rejection of Christ".[10]

Jesus himself connects his going away with the coming of the Spirit and the building of his Church. In his Body, the Church, wherein the Holy Spirit dwells, he intends to remain as the source of all grace. Hence, this Body, the Church, becomes the condition or the embodiment of our restored relationship with Christ and our entrance into the kingdom of God. Christ, absent from the universal human community, is made present again through the resurrection in the Church, his Body on earth.

The weighty consequence of this fact is significantly expressed by St. Thomas: "The grace of Christ comes to us not through human nature but through the *personal action* of Christ himself." [11] In present-day terms this means that the source of Christ's grace is not fellow-creaturehood in and by itself, but fellow-creaturehood with Christ, who, while absent since his death from the horizon of our experience, means to remain present among us,

[10] P. Schoonenberg, "Natuur en zondenval," in *Tijdschr. v. Theol.* 2 (1962), pp. 199-200; see also E. Schillebeeckx, *Christ, the Sacrament of the Encounter with God* (New York, 1963), pp. 40-46.

[11] *Summa Theologiae,* III, q.8, a.2, ad 1.

but post-paschally, in virtue of the Spirit of God, in his Body, the Church.

As the Body of our Lord, the Church forms the living link with Christ—horizontally, with the Jesus of history, who arose and appeared to the apostles; vertically, with the Lord of glory, thanks to the Spirit that dwells in the whole community of the Church in its hierarchical function, its preaching, its sacraments. Because of Christ's fellowship with us the universal human fellowship, too, takes on a deepened meaning, and the boundaries between mankind and the Church begin to blur.

IV

FLUIDITY OF THE BOUNDARIES BETWEEN THE CHURCH AND MANKIND

The history of salvation, then, deals with one covenant that has passed through two phases, or a twofold *dispositio*. An absolutely new situation has been created in the plan of salvation by Christ's death and resurrection. Now the further question arises: What is the relationship between the universal People of God, coextensive with mankind, and the Church, in which the People of God has become the Body of our Lord?

The *locus theologicus* of all reflection on the faith and, consequently, of the theology of the relationships between the Church and the world, is the historical advent of salvation in Jesus Christ: the man Jesus who is to us the absolute and gratuitous presence of God. In Christ and through him, human existence has become the objective expression of God's absolute communication of himself to man and, by the same token, the objective expression of the human response to that total divine gift. As a corollary of that fact, the human condition in its historical setting has become the concrete matter and space of the historical manifestation of man's God-related life in Christ. The human existence of Christ, taken with all its determinisms and all its human implications, is the *personal* life of God, the Son.

This means that the entire temporal dimension and the una-bridged reality we call profane can be assumed into a God-related life, given that in the Son the eternal has presented itself person-ally within temporal and terrestrial realities. The very definition of the hypostatic union is exactly that. This also reveals the fact that thanks to Christ all of human history is swathed in God's love; it is assumed into the absolute and gratuitous presence of the mystery of God. The worldly and the temporal remain worldly and temporal; they are not sacralized but sanctified by that pres-ence, that is, by the God-centered life of Christ and of his faithful.

Everyone will agree that our human existence is immersed in unfathomable mystery, although the way of saying so may vary infinitely. In her revelation-through-the-Word, the Church merely clarifies for the benefit of all mankind the reality of the mystery's absolute presence in Christ; it proclaims that this mystery has drawn closer to us, not only in some mystical and interior inti-macy, but also through the medium of a palpable and visible historical reality. The whole kerygma and all of Christian dogma can be summarized in that fundamental affirmation: beginning with the Trinity, the incarnation, the life of grace, but also includ-ing the Church with her ministry, worship, preaching, sacraments as well as collective and individual eschatology.

Word-revelation, of which the Church is the herald, only un-folds the implications of that absolute and gratuitous presence which, as revelations-reality, is already present in the lives of men, even prior to their historical encounter with the phenomenon "Church". Moreover, the free acceptance of the mystery's abso-lute and gratuitous presence is the very substance of what we call theologal or God-related faith. To believe is to have confidence in this mystery thus present; it means trusting in him in spite of everything and under all circumstances. That affirmation strikes me as of the utmost importance because what is implied is that the acceptance of real human existence, concretely taken with all its responsibilities, is in truth an act of God-centered faith:

for Christ has shown us, by living it, that human existence taken concretely—not in the abstract—was for him, precisely in his human condition steeped as it was in the mystery, the objective expression of his communion with the Father in the *Dynamis* of the Holy Spirit and for the benefit of his fellowmen.

Here is what this brief analysis shows us:

1. Within the Church of Christ the absolute and gratuitous presence of the mystery becomes an explicit epiphany, historically and humanly observable—both as a reality and as a task to be accomplished.

2. This concentrated ecclesial manifestation of God merely explicates that which in fact and at its own level is going on in all of human existence, even if the subject is not aware of it, namely, the gratuitous presence of the mystery, which is an active, an operative presence.

From this viewpoint, the incarnation teaches us that the entire human reality may ferry divine grace and can be assumed into a God-centered life. Day-to-day human life with its worldly concerns for human advancement is the area wherein normal Christian life must develop; the explicit and ecclesial expression of that selfsame communion with God shall indeed be the fountainhead and the driving force of the expression of Christian life in the world. St. Paul told us as much in a masterful though negative manner: "Neither death, nor life, nor angels, nor principalities, nor things present, nor things to come, nor powers, nor height, nor depth, nor any other creature will be able to separate us from the love of God, which is in Christ Jesus our Lord" (Rom. 8, 38-39). What does it all mean if not that Christianity is upheld by faith in the absolute and gratuitous presence of God within Christ as well as by the fact that we must accept human history and our entire earthly life as a reality steeped and swaddled in God's love? Improving the world whenever we improve ourselves, we are always in the presence of and beneath the wings of the mystery who gives himself freely.

While respecting the worldly and earthly significance of the reality we call the world, this outlook gives it a profoundly theological meaning. This is what the world is: the profane, earthly and temporal reality with structures all its own, with its special and immediate end, but which, in Christ, is assumed into the absolute and gratuitous presence of God. In saying this one should beware of imagining the world as some static, immobile reality. Planet earth is the material given to man with which to fashion a human world, a dwelling-place worthy of man. Of course man's world has the mark of the creature upon it; moreover, as everything else common to man, it is a world wrought by sin. The construction of the world and the promotion of peoples remain a finite task, the work of men, and as such it shares in the ambiguity of all that is human. This world is creature, non-God. To say this is to affirm the secularity of earthly tasks. Indeed, creation is a divine act that situates realities within their respective spheres; and contrary to the mythological legends held by the contemporaries of ancient Israel, the Bible refers to that divine act, in Genesis, as desacralizing and unmystifying the world, handing it over to itself, into the hands of man for God's glory. This means that as a result of the divine act of sustained creation, the history of mankind will assert itself as the progressive and prolonged desacralization of earthly structures and functions.

But that is only one facet of a far richer and more profound reality: since God created so as to bestow himself to man and to be, he himself, present in a gratuitous and redemptive manner, in our brother, Jesus the Anointed. This means that in the plan of salvation the concrete world, by definition, is an *implicit Christianity;* it is an objective, non-sacral but saintly and sanctified expression of mankind's communion with the living God; whereas the Church *qua* institution of salvation, with her explicit creed, her worship and sacraments, is the direct and sacral expression of that identical communion—she is the *separata a mundo.*

To speak of the relationships between the Church and the world does not mean therefore that a dialogue is to be launched between the strictly Christian dimension of our human life and its distinctly non-Christian dimension; nor is it a question of conducting a dialogue between the religious and the profane, between the supernatural and the natural or intra-worldly—it is rather a dialogue between *two complementary, authentically Christian expressions* of one and the same God-related life concealed in the mystery of Christ, namely, the *ecclesial* expression (in the strict sense of the word) and the *worldly* expression of that identically same life, internalized within human life through man's free acceptance of grace. In other words, the *implicitly* Christian and the *explicitly* Christian dimension of the same God-related life, that is, of human life hidden in God's absolute and gratuitous presence.[11a] In that context, this is what is meant by implicit Christianity; it is the human, earthly and profane reality assumed in its secularity into the God-related life which it proceeds to express objectively, even when that God-related life remains anonymous and implicit. Earthly reality will at the same time share in the first fruits of eschatological grace and in the advent of the kingdom of God. Within that God-centered life, albeit anonymous, the construction of the world and the promotion of peoples, those two great hopes of mankind on earth, become an activity which is not only intentionally but intrinsically relevant to the kingdom of God.

It is evident that the ultimate eschatological perfection of all earthly values completely transcends the temporal construction of this world, precisely because it is an absolute and gratuitous

---

[11a] It is obvious that in so saying I speak of the state of implicit Christianity as such, realizing that the individual can shut himself away from grace. God is the sole judge of man's conscience. One does not therefore affirm that all non-Christians are by the mere fact implicitly Christians, just as one does not maintain that every member of the Church is an authentic Christian. Nevertheless the redemptive grace of "Christus Victor" is more powerful than the fragility of human freedom.

perfection; but nevertheless, by virtue of its assumption into God-related life, harbinger of the *vita venturi saeculi,* the world of earthly values will participate in that mystery of eternal life, as we are told by the dogma of the resurrection of the flesh and by the kerygma of the new earth.

Unequivocally, God loves man; and the being called man is not some abstract "human nature" but a flesh-and-blood being who, together with his fellowmen, takes the fate of the world and of mankind into his own hands; he is a being who, by humanizing the world humanizes himself. It is this historical, real being whom God loves. Every single human and worldly reality is therefore implied in God's absolute and gratuitous presence. This conveys a sense of the eternal and, therefore, of the irrevocable to the construction of the world and the promotion of the advancement of peoples.

Although it is solely due to his *capacitas gratiae* that man is the object of grace, the very being who, upon transcending his own self is assumed into theologal intimacy with God and shares in the eternal life—that being is none other than man, all of man as he really and historically exists, committed to this world.

In the past, a dualistic anthropological conception misled Christians into considering grace and redemption as a matter for God and the soul of man to deal with, so much so that the whole range of earthly life and of human responsibility for the terrestrial future of mankind seemed to be relegated to the fringe of Christianity; one ran the risk of disregarding the truly Christian value of building the world and of promoting the advancement of peoples, thereby relinquishing the chore to those who called themselves non-Christians. How easy it is to discern in that behavior one of the many factors through which the institutional Church alienated men from herself.

When we connect now the things which were said about the one signification of the Church with that which is called "implicit

Christianity", we arrive at new explicitations concerning the relation "Church and World."

The acts of Christ in glory are the acts of the whole Christ, the integral Christ in and with his Body, the Church. Hence, what the Church as such does, is done also by the glorified Christ together with the Spirit, his Spirit. What is Christian, therefore, is also ecclesial: the qualifications are inseparably and organically united.

However much Jesus, as the Lord, transcends his Body, the Church, his immanence in the Church is coextensive with his transcendence. He transcends the Church through his immanence in it. That he transcends the boundaries of his Body, the Church, means that his free self-giving reaches out from within the Church to all who are not yet visible members of the Church. This implies that he is active among those who have not yet been historically confronted with the Church, but also that this activity of his is equally an activity of his Body, the Church. The bond with Christ, forged by this activity is, even when not explicitly seen as such, *ipso facto* an equally strong bond with the Church. Consequently, the Church represents the source of redemption also for that portion of mankind that has not yet experienced and availed itself of her in her peculiar historical form.

Seen in this perspective, the real interval separating the Church as such from mankind becomes less pronounced. The Church is actively present even where her adequate ecclesial form has not yet appeared. The contrast between the Church and mankind cannot be equated with an opposition between Church and non-Church. There is, moreover, much in her own life that is "non-ecclesial", just as in the collective life of mankind there is much that is ecclesial. In the strict sense, of course, the Church is mankind insofar as it willingly places itself under Christ's influence through faith and baptism, and "helps its unbelief" at the common table of the eucharist.

Perhaps it is better not to give the name "Church" to that portion of mankind that is anonymously Christian and in which the Church is anonymously present. This phenomenon might be called a "pre-Church"; but even against this, various objections might be brought. In the proper sense of the word, the Church is the saving revelation, the explicitly Christian realization of our Lord's activity among all mankind—the *koinonía* of men with one another in the acceptance of God and baptism in Christ, which is the efficacious sign of the call of those not yet in the Church.

On the other hand, anonymous Christianity—and its existence must be taken as a fact—not least because of its hopeful trust in the triumphant grace of Christ's redemption ("I have overcome the world") is an anonymity that inwardly demands a fitting sacramental visibility. Because the worldwide activity of Christ's grace is carried out in and through the Church, since his "going away" is related to the Church's post-paschal reality as the Body of our Lord, in virtue of the Spirit of God, this very grace is essentially "Church founding". Where the Church is at work as grace—and as such it is coextensive with mankind and therefore with universal fellowship—something of the *Corpus Mysticum* is brought to visible realization, though in a veiled manner. Because this grace takes on particular, historical, visible forms in the Church, its appearance bears witness to the fact that wherever it is operative (and that is wherever human history is in process of realization), it has an inward leaning toward historical manifestation, *i.e.,* toward ecclesial explicitness.

This process can be observed in human history. Beyond the pale of the concretely situated, real Church, this grace will express itself, as a result of the unrecognized bond with Christ and his Church, in widely varying human interpretations—whether in other religious forms, or in so-called "secular" institutions, whose explicit form is inadequate to express their true purpose. Failure to grasp the proper meaning of this deepest feeling latent in the restless life of mankind is no indication that the difference between mankind and the Church is merely one of "knowing explicitly" and "knowing implicitly". For it is only in self-expression that man reaches full self-consciousness. Whatever is experienced without being recognized is a fragile datum until it finds its way to authentic self-expression. And this is more than a question of mere knowledge.

Without the God-given ecclesial form and expression of this deepest core of life in Christ, this experience remains a "light hidden under a bushel", a flickering flame ready to be quenched by the weakest draught. The properly ecclesial milieu is where the word of God's forgiveness is heard, where baptism is administered and the eucharist celebrated, where there is the faith that nothing can separate us from the Lord and that for men there is no absolute solitude because God is with us. This milieu, which believers, the faithful, jointly constitute, is vitally necessary for the breakthrough of what grace effects silently and anonymously in human life. But the Church's special importance as a sign and revelation demands that she return again and again to the sources of biblical authenticity and show herself in forms that clearly and simply manifest her authenticity.

Thanks, therefore, to Christ's historical coming there is in living humanity a kind of built-in compass pointing to the Church. Her missionary activity is merely the counterpart of this. This pointing to the Church, or mankind's need of her in the concrete, and, on the other hand, her going out to mankind, are both visible forms of the one operative salvation which our Lord is in the Spirit of God, *Pneuma Theoû*. In both, Jesus the Christ visits his messianic community that he acquired upon the cross to prepare for himself his eschatological bride without spot unto the glory of God the Father.

The anonymous Church that is the work of Christ's Spirit and of his Body, the explicit Church vitally joined to him, will become manifest through the Spirit, as his Body, incorporated through baptism into his death and resurrection, as a visible sign both of the eschatological Man, Jesus Christ, and of what human life is concretely—namely, a deep and painful suffering, an existence ending in death, coupled with the unquenchable hope that this is not the last word about mankind. In Christ's *kenôsis* and *hypsôsis,* in his final humiliation and his exaltation, the destiny of human life is exemplified. The enduring struggle for life in mankind, hoping against all hope, is the nameless echo of this fact: there is here more than mere secularity, even though it is expressed perhaps in a purely secular fashion.

The boundaries between the Church and mankind are fluid not merely in the Church's direction, but also, it may be said, in the direction of mankind and the world. The present-day process toward desacralization and secularization points to the fact that what was earlier felt to be a specialty of the Church—helping those of slender means, works of charity and the like—has nowadays become "desacralized" as state relief measures for humanity within a secular vision, and is now an accepted feature of mankind at large. What had earlier taken the form of specific activities of the Church, in its precise sense, has now become in many ways an accepted expression of man's life in and for the world.

This osmosis from the Church to the world knows no final point on earth because here below the old aeon and the new continue to co-exist. The fact that the communion of men coincides with the communion of saints is, when manifest, a heavenly, not an earthly fact. The blurring of the boundaries between the Church and mankind can never abolish the dialectical tension between the two. This tension, however, does not destroy either the dynamic of the world's tendency to become ecclesial or the Church's tendency to sanctify the secular. The latter process, however, is a holy secularization arising from the transcendent community with God in Christ. Whoever forgets this would have the Church in the long run dissolve into something like UNO or UNESCO.

All this has been expressed by St. Paul in his own way and in the framework of his ancient world picture. Christ by his death and glorification has fulfilled "all things"—"all things in heaven and on earth", "visible and invisible", all created reality (Eph. 1, 10; Col. 1, 16-20). H. Schlier, the biblical exegete, in his commentary on Ephesians comments rightly upon this point: "There is no sphere of being that is not also the Church's sphere. The Church is fundamentally directed to the universe. Her boundaries are those of the universe. There is no realization of Christ's dominion without the Church or outside her, no "fulfill-ment" apart from her. The way in which the universe grows to-ward Christ is the way the Church grows. There are areas, to be sure, that are opposed to "fulfillment" through the Church; but ultimately the reason is that they are filled with themselves." [12]

St. Paul says this plainly: "God has placed all things under his feet, and has given him, exalted above all, as Head to the Church, which is his Body, the fullness of him who fulfills all in all" (Eph. 1, 22f.). It is through the Church that the fulfillment of all existence and all reality is achieved.[13] Eschatologically, Church and mankind coincide fully.

V

UNITY OF CREATION, REDEMPTION AND GROWTH OF THE CHURCH

The Church and mankind, then, are coming closer together; and yet the undeniable boundary remains between them because

[12] H. Schlier, "Die Kirche nach dem Briefe an die Epheser," in *Die Zeit der Kirche* (Freiburg im Br., 1956), p. 69.

[13] Schlier has the following acute comment on this passage in Saint Paul: "The Church is the *Pleroma* of Christ. This means the plenitude, fulfilled by him and in its turn fulfilling, of him who has fulfilled all things and continues to do so. In her (the Church's) plenitude, all is enclosed and so this all becomes itself that plenitude which is the Church" (*ibid.,* p. 170).

of Christ's post-paschal "building of the Church upon the Rock".[14] It now remains to clarify a dogmatic insight in which creation and the bestowal of grace, redemption and the building of the Church are all seen together in the sublime unity of God's covenant with men.

Grace is God's absolute self-communication to men; it is the personal sharing of life with God—Father, Son, and Holy Spirit. That even in the pre-Christian era grace could only be trinitarian, we only know in the light of the historical mystery of Christ. It is in him that this fundamental aspect of the whole life of grace first becomes explicit. There is a close connection between him and grace. The fact that the trinitarian character of grace, imparted before his coming, remained implicit and anonymous leads to the question whether the anonymous character of this trinitarian grace is not due to the fact that man's existence was originally orientated to Christ, and that this obviously had to remain implicit. An analysis of the trinitarian character of grace as well as of its postponed revelation in Christ shows that its original conferment and God's establishment of mankind as his People were the consequence of man's creation in view of Christ. "Adam's" creation was implicitly directed toward Christ, and because of this, grace was bestowed upon him.[15] In other words, human existence in the concrete is itself a messianic prophecy pointing to him who is to come. The task to form a true *communio* among men as the essential task of a community of *persons* is a prophecy of the coming of Christ's Mystical Body, the Church. Thus, by another and perhaps more radical way we come to a conclusion at least materially the same as Karl Rahner's

[14] The thought of this article will be taken up again in CONCILIUM and applied to the problem of membership in the Churches, in connection with the pluralism of the Christian Church communities.

[15] I have attempted to develop this in detail in "Die Heiligung des Namen Gottes durch die Menschenliebe Jesu des Christus," in *Gott in Welt* (Festgabe für K. Rahner, Freiburg, 1964), esp. pp. 73-90.

who speaks of mankind in its entirety as the (faithful or unfaithful) People of God, and considers membership of this People a constitutive element of our concrete humanity.[16] Therefore, in the concrete, every free human act is one that works toward salvation or perdition. But it seems to me that the manner in which we arrive at this insight sheds a clearer light on mankind's objectively new situation since the death and resurrection of Christ.

Surely this new situation makes it obvious that salvation is conferred upon the People of God, not as such, but insofar as it has become the Body of Christ. This implies that since the appearance of the mystery of Christ in history at least the faithful People of God, in virtue of his sole saving power at work in his Body, the Church, becomes the expression of a *desiderium ecclesiae*. The basis of this should be clear from what has been thus far presented here, but it may help to clarify it further.

Creation in view of Christ, which includes the gift of grace, means that since creation all mankind carries within itself and anonymously this ecclesial orientation as a grace that is accepted or rejected. We may say, then, that it is always within and for a People of God that man's religious life is fulfilled, whether this People be mankind as yet unspecified or Israel, in which messianic humanity began to manifest itself more clearly, or the People of God redeemed by Christ, with its features sharply drawn and constituted as the Church.[17] The human community, insofar as it is created with this orientation toward Christ is an early rough-draft of the Church that is to come. But it is no more than that. For the appearance of Jesus in history and his exclusion from the human community created a completely new situation. It is as the Risen One that he built his Church and set it visibly

---

[16] K. Rahner, "Die Gliedschaft in der Kirche nach der Lehre de Enzyklika Pius XII, *Mystici Corporis*," in *Schr. z. Theol.* 2 (Einsiedeln, 1955), pp. 7-94.

[17] E. Schillebeeckx, *Personale Begegnung mit Gott: Eine Antwort an John A. T. Robinson* (Mainz, 1964), pp. 78f.

among men as a community with its peculiar sacramental community structure, with its hierarchical function, with its service of the Word.

This absolutely new fact in salvation history restricts the universal application of this reality of God's People as coextensive with mankind. On the other hand, this new fact lifts that reality into a new dimension and turns its implicit acceptance into a *votum ecclesiae*. The anonymously Christian portion of mankind now becomes for the first time a true *votum ecclesiae,* precisely because of Christ's universally operative action *in* the Church to the benefit of all mankind.[18]

Christ's Church, then, is not so much the last phase of the interior development of God's People as it comes into ever clearer view in visible form, although this aspect cannot be denied. Rather, Christ's historical redemptive work with its post-paschal fruit, the Church, recapitulates in his death and resurrection the People of God created from of old in view of him, and *constitutes* that People as the *votum ecclesiae*. Hence, we can say: *Extra ecclesiam nulla salus:* apart from Christ and his Body there is no salvation.

At the same time we must say that the Church here on earth has not yet reached the perfection of what she ought to be. This was acutely formulated by Origen: *"Ho kosmos tou kosmou he ekklesia":* man's world brought to actual perfection, to order— to peace and *communio*—this is the Church.[19] The Church carries within herself the principles and the incipient reality of this

---

[18] Be it noted that I do not claim that *all* those who do not belong to a church are *per se* anonymous Christians, just as we do not maintain that all church members are authentic Christians. I only say that such an anonymous Christianity is a genuine possibility, and, considering the abounding power of grace, a reality in the case of many. We do not wish, nor are we able, to affirm their number. We know well the essential ambiguity of human freedom: it is a potentiality for good and for evil. But our confidence in God is greater than that ambiguity!

[19] See A. Auer, "Kirche und Welt," in *Mysterium Kirche* II (Salzburg, 1962), pp. 492f.

peace in virtue of the fact that she, the fruit of Christ's redemption, is his Body in this world.

In and through that Body he, now in glory, carries on his universal activity in the Spirit. The Church in human history, then, is, as token for all the world, the forerunner of eschatological salvation. Hence, her apostolic duty; hence, the constant demand daily to orientate herself anew at the wellsprings of Holy Scripture, especially at this time when the face of the world and of man is fundamentally altering.

VI

THE CHURCH AS FELLOWSHIP TO BE REALIZED

The blurring of the enduring boundaries between the Church and mankind can also be explained more clearly through the Church's inner structure. In the one Church of Christ we may distinguish two different, though not opposed, dialectical aspects: the one, of the Church as a community guided by the Spirit of God active in the apostolic office of the episcopacy throughout the world; the other, of the same Church guided by the Spirit of God active in every individual's conscience.

This latter activity of the Spirit, and hence of individual Christians, also effects the building of the Church, especially in the midst of the world and of ordinary everyday things. This is where they are to be found who have not yet joined the Church community explicitly. Here, too, the building of the Church retains a kind of hidden character. Because this is a non-hierarchical activity, which is just as much the work of the Holy Spirit in Christian consciences, there really is an active building of the Church by her members in the midst of the so-called "profane" world, where the hierarchical Church is not present. A genuine, but even more veiled manifestation of this reality, moreover, is the genesis of the Church in the world that is Christian without the name. It can be recognized for what it is only in the light of Christ and the visible Church.

If, therefore, we would inquire into the pregnant characteristics that mark out the anonymously Christian Church which, because of what she is, longs for the moment when she can appear in her own ecclesial manifestation, we should not consider the fellowship or brotherhood among men in general, but with the special qualification which Jesus himself indicated. This qualification is love, a love that reaches out to the *mikroi,* the little ones, and to the *elachistoi,* the least of men, to help them for the reason that Jesus calls them "My brethren" (Matt. 25, 31-36). It is in respect to their practice of this love that Church members and non-Church members alike are to be judged at the end of time (Matt. 25, 35-45): "What you have done to the least of my brethren, you have done to me" (Matt. 25, 40). "I was hungry and you gave me to eat; I was thirsty and you gave me to drink; I was a stranger and you welcomed me" (Matt. 25, 35f.). "What you have failed to do for the least of these, you have failed to do for me" (Matt. 25, 45).

In modern terms this might be expressed thus: Your failure to help the underdeveloped countries is failing Christ himself. The help you extend to them, not from political motives, but out of pure brotherhood and fellowship, is authentic Christianity. Self-sacrifice to the extreme was the messianic act by which Christ founded his Church. Where men follow in his footsteps on the way of self-sacrifice, without even knowing perhaps whose steps they are, they are working to establish the Church, the community in Christ. The parable of the Good Samaritan teaches us, with a certain amount of sarcasm directed at those who are "in the Church", that everyone who assists anyone whom he finds in need and helps him superabundantly, with the luxury of extravagant love, is actively establishing the *koinonía.* He makes of the man he helps, his neighbor and brother.

The activity that establishes the Church which is, even without the name, Christian, goes outside and beyond the limits of the official Church, which is sociologically situated and clearly visible in history—the Church of those who acknowledge Christ and share the table of the eucharist. This activity exceeds the official Church's limits even in such a way that this superabundant love, however clearly visible in the Church's saints, is not, historically and *per se,* necessarily realized by practicing Christians. And yet the Church is truly established only where love makes men brothers, because the active love that establishes her is the core of her being. It was to preserve that core that Christ established an official hierarchy, which he assists in a special manner in order to preserve his People in one community of love and hope founded upon one faith in him. Ultimately, however, the Church is not a matter of this hierarchy but of the People of God and the active love that establishes her. And for her, the hierarchy, although in the *modus* of Christian authority, has a function of service.

Outside the visible community of Jesus, then, the establishment of the Church is accomplished primarily by surrender to one's fellowmen in unselfish love. Concretely, our fellow-creatures are a token of God's grace, a sacramental sign of his saving will. Such they are only because created in Christ and for the sake of him who is the constitutive sign of God's saving will. The universal sacramentality of fellow-creaturehood is not destroyed because of the perfect sacramental form of Christ's fellow-creaturehood, nor is it, so to say, translated into the formal structure of the visible Church. On the contrary, because of the appearance of the Man, Jesus Christ the Son of God, in history, the sacramental power of the grace of fellowship can be realized in its full meaning now for the first time. It is realized in him and for him. The general sacramental feature of fellowship is made concrete only in the community that is called the Church. And the seven sacraments, the preaching, the worship, the hierarchy's guidance—all these are but the highest point of crystallization of the stake the Church has in our fellowmen.

The Church, therefore, will appear as a sign among men, actually drawing and inviting them, only when the love of her members for humankind becomes concretely and historically visible here and now, and is no longer confined to those particular climactic moments in which at present Christ places his grace in a concentrated manner. It is just during the Second Vatican Council that out of the deliberations on the nature of the Church there has come a desire to include in the schema a consideration of the active presence of church members in the world. The schema which is shortly to become the Constitution, *De Ecclesia,* cries out from the heart for schema xvii.

On all these grounds we cannot relegate the Church's significance for the unchurched to some kind of "representative function" that would dispense them from the superabundant love and redeem them by "substitution", that is, by the overflowing love which is at least present in Christ's Church. In an authentically Christian perspective, vicariousness and mediation never stand for substitution, but for a prototypical reality which gives of its abundance *in order that* others, by virtue of the grace they have received, may be enabled themselves to achieve what had already been done by the prototype. In this sense the Church exists in the strength of Christ's Spirit for the good of all men. But equally, the operation of Christ's grace among men through the Church must retain a visible form, especially in its apostolic activity. In the Church's confrontation with mankind in history her members must be living examples and "types" of this overflowing love and manifest their willingness to give up their personal lives in the service of others.

VII

Secular and Sacral Realization of the Church's Holiness

The problem posed at the beginning of this essay has found some answer, it is hoped, in the course of our investigation. There is obviously going on throughout mankind a process of bringing things into the Church, and in the Church, correspondingly, there is a process of secularization that conveys sanctity. Within the inviolable limits set by the Word, the sacrament, and the office—and all those are forms of *service*—the boundaries between the Church and mankind are blurred. It is in the positive encounter with Christ in his Church that the most complete form of Christianity that may be realized is objectively offered to us.

The Church, then, must be a really habitable home, and her mission is to bring this to pass in every age in ever differing ways. Complete religion has an explicitly Christian and ecclesial practical expression. Because of this, Christianity, however involved it is in our everyday cares and tasks and all our secular activity, has a special sacral space set apart from secular developments and from culture, within which we grow in intimacy with God. Here we are simply together with God in Christ. Now, on a merely human level silence forms a part of discourse and social intercourse, though in and for itself it has no meaning; it has meaning only as a function of fellowship. It is necessary in order to make contact between men human and to keep it so—to humanize it. It is silence that makes speech personal. Without it, dialogue is impossible. But in a revealed religion, silence with God has a value in itself and for its own sake, just because God is God. Failure to recognize the value of mere being with God, as the Beloved, without doing anything, is to gouge the heart out of Christianity.

Our whole immersion in the world of men and things penetrates also into our communion with God, not as mere distraction, but essentially. We cannot tell God that we love or desire to love him except with words, concepts and pictures taken from our human environment. Moreover, our communion with God is not individualism, for our prayer would be insincere—not prayer at all—if we did not pray: "Our Father, . . ." or if in our prayer we forgot God's kingdom and our fellowman.

Christianity means not only communion with God in the concrete milieu of Christ in his Church, but also *working* with the living God, with the Father "who is ever active" (John 5, 17) both in the Church and in the world. Religion is primarily personal intercourse with God—the living God, who is the Creator of men and things, all of which he offers to us for humanization. Therefore, our living relationship with our neighbor and with the world is not only cultural, but also religious.

Agape embraces God and men. Love of God cannot and must not be separated from love of men. Christian love for the neighbor means that we—God and I—love *my* fellowman. While in natural human love, God is present only in silence as the transcendent Third, my Christian *caritas* toward my fellows is just as much love, but a love lived in communion with God. And so the Christian loves his fellowman with the same love as that with which he loves God and with which both he and his fellowmen are loved by God. In Christ alone do we learn the proper meaning of "being a man for the sake of others", although secular and human experience will teach us how we must express this fellowship in concrete situations.

But, however ecclesial the explicit expression of religion and Christianity may be, the working out of our Christian character must needs take shape in the ordinary daily dealings in and with the world and our fellowmen. The sincerity of our personal dealings with God, of our Christianity and ecclesial status must therefore be tested constantly by the authenticity of our fellowship, our genuine love of men. The source of this Christian love of the neighbor, however, lies in our personal assimilation of those ways of dealing with God which Christ himself has given us: hearing the Word of God, familiarity with Holy Scripture, the common celebration of the Church's sacramental liturgy. In our world, then, authentic Christianity has both a *sacred* and a corresponding *secular* milieu. In everything he does, by acceptance or refusal, man brings about salvation or perdition.

We must be close to God, not merely in church, in prayer and the sacraments, in Scripture reading—in a word, in the sacred forms of religion—but also in our secular and human relationships and in our everyday tasks. Then we may say with serenity that there are different ways of being Christian. Some will bring their interior relationship with God to fulfillment chiefly in sacral forms, thereby stressing the fact that the Church is "not of this world". Others will express their Christianity particularly in secular activities, in "secular sanctity", and so will stress the fact that the Christian faith is not an ideological structure superimposed upon human life.

But these are emphases of the one Christian life which is immanent in this world precisely because it is transcendent. For what has been said here about the universal relationship between mankind and the Church is also valid for the individual Christian. The unrecognized genuine witness of the Christian in this profane world finds the source of its strength in that explicit Christianity which is shaped by active participation in the life of the Word and of the Sacrament of "Christ's Church".

MICHAEL NOVAK

Born in 1933 in Johnstown, Pennsylvania. He received his A.B. in philosophy in 1956 at Stonehill College and his degree in theology in 1958 at Gregorian University, Rome. In 1960 he pursued studies in the philosophy of religion at Harvard University. He is an essayist and novelist. In addition to many articles in philosophical and theological reviews, he is the author of *The Tiber was Silver* (1961); *A New Generation: American and Catholic* (1964); *The Open Church: Vatican II, Act II* (1964); *The Experience of Marriage* (1964). He has edited the Catholic quarterly *The Current,* and has written scripts for television about Teilhard de Chardin and Romano Guardini.

Michael Novak / *Johnstown, Pa., U.S.A.*

Diversity of Structures and Freedom within Structures of the Church

Toward what new structures should the evolution of the Church be directed in order to enter into the mainstream of the life of men? The present structure of the Catholic Church seems too univocal, particular and uniform. In order to be more human, the Church must be more catholic. Catholics must learn to stress the importance of the concrete, the particular, the different, in a word, the diversity within the Church. Given modern communications, unity of spirit is more easily attained; the maintenance of spiritual diversity, even within the same faith, requires intelligence and care.

Of course, there already exists much diversity among Catholics. Catholics in England and in Italy do not mean the same things when they speak of *law and order*. The French *liberté* is not the American *freedom*. For the German and for the Latin American, *organization* and *authority* do not have the same meaning. The life of the layman in the Congo is different from the life of the layman in Canada. We cannot talk about "new structures in the Church" unless we recognize that the human race is seriously and blessedly diverse. Even fundamental words like *structure* itself call to mind different images, different relationships and different attitudes in the different languages of the world. Each of us—and the regional culture of each—is concrete, finite, special. There is not now—and, let us hope, never will be—a universal standardized "man". The ideal of a universal abstract type, of a form which all are to strive to fit, of a uniform structure for all, is a seriously mistaken and dangerous ideal.

In every discussion of "new structures" there is implied a periodization of history: of what has been, is becoming and will be. Perhaps it will be useful to make the hidden theory of this article explicit. In the past, the structure of social action derived its strength from the community, from the *Gemeinschaft*. There are many who interpret the modern age as a crisis of community, a crisis of fragmented society in which individuals are adrift in painful isolation. To such commentators, the fact that questions of moral choice and moral destiny have been differentiated down to the level of the individual person, without a "sense of community" to give these individuals moral support, is the deep tragedy of modern life. I would argue, on the other hand, that it is precisely this differentiation that is the glory of modern life, because it opens out before each of us the radical human trial.

However we interpret the value of modern life, surely the fact is plain enough. Social and communal pressures (whether from family, State, Church, economic order or cultural traditions) are less and less important in the actual decisions made by individuals about the content of their lives and their actions. Everywhere we hear talk about "the breakup of the old order", the "lack of respect for old values and traditions", and the rest. Moreover, this process appears to be carried to its farthest extremes precisely in those countries that are generally regarded as "most advanced". It is for this reason that this process seems to be the fruitful key to the interpretation of cultural evolution; the process has many stages analogous to each other. In the new countries of Africa, in the restless nations of Latin America, in the Soviet Union of 1918, in present-day Germany or Sweden, the breakdown of the old order is always different according as the old order is different. At each successive change, more choices are left to the individual.

There are many complaints today, of course, about the "mass man". I think the critics of the new mass man are deceived by external appearances—the sameness of urban buildings, the ubiquity of the same radio broadcasts, newspapers and television images. To be sure, in every age there are many men who refuse to act decisively, who drift with the current of their community. The peasants and townsmen of yesterday (and they are living still in enclaves all around us) appear to produce as many such men as our modern cities. Nevertheless, in too many quarters there lingers a nostalgia for the old forms of "community", for the old pressures of a group in which the individual knows what is expected of him and what benefits are due him. Instead, today's individual must choose his own associations, his own affiliations, his own allegiances.

Is it not the point of critics that the life of the masses seems "formless", and that they are thus susceptible of being roused by demagogues? A truer view, at least in more stable countries, is that individuals are grouped in many voluntary associations, pressure groups, clubs, Churches, etc. A system of free associations is complex, but it is not formless. Such a system represents a spiritual victory of great importance for the human race; it maximizes the range of choices within which the individual works out his destiny. Our shortsightedness or our nostalgia can lead us to turn this victory into an ancient defeat.

Two versions of such an ancient defeat should be mentioned. First, in the name of the deficiencies of the old order (surely obvious to all), Marxism replaces the evolution toward the differentiation of individuals with a new set of group pressures, sometimes of the most violent sort. Secondly, "Americanization" (such as it is understood in Gaullist France and among European intellectuals generally) would likewise mean the end of the differentiation of individual moral destiny, unless it is only a myth, generated by a misunderstanding of American life.

In the countries generally thought of as "more advanced", it is precisely the degree of differentiation allowed to individuals—and not industrial superiority—which is the most profound measure of their development. Never in history have young people had so many avenues of differentiation as are now open to them. Where they will live, where they will work, how often they will change jobs, what they will believe, with whom they will associate, how involved they become in issues (and in *which* issues)—neither family, nor Church, nor employer, nor party, nor tradition can determine. The *malaise* felt among the young in such countries is not that of having their future predetermined by society or by some organization to which they are bound; it is that of having an "open" future, of not having enough guidance, of having too many possibilities. They must choose even their personal standard of values, their own measure of what constitutes a human life. Faced by so many choices, no one of which compels assent, they are afflicted with *ennui* and powerlessness.

The roots of this *malaise,* however, are fundamentally healthy, sound and praiseworthy. The sickness arises from the too-sudden advent of the very freedom for which the human race has been striving. Freedom, as Dostoievski forewarned, is so terrifying a burden that few can tolerate it. The young are burdened by a freedom their elders cannot teach them how to use. All attempts to restore a "sense of values", to restore a "community", are only steps backward into the very social pressures from which the young feel liberated. The fact that liberty is terrifying has surprised us. But then such liberty, on so large a scale, is new on the face of the earth, and few generations have ever known what it is to be born with it. It is no wonder that in many places the younger generation seems already older than its years.

If this periodization is correct—and much evidence seems to support it—then, any assumption that "new structures" in the Church must try to recreate the community of the past, in whatever new styles or by whatever new methods, is seriously in error. The search for community is reversion to a lesser value, to an earlier stage of cultural development. What I mean by this needs to be made clear.

To argue for ever-increasing room for differentiation is not to argue for "rugged individualism", economic, personal or spiritual. It is not to argue that "the soul is alone before God", or that men should live "each for himself". It is not to support 19th-century Anglo-Saxon individualism, *laissez-faire* or utilitarianism. It is not to support cultural or individual relativism. It is, on the other hand, to allow an *environment,* in which such aberrations can exist, for the sake of a deeper kind of freedom. It is to allow the individual person "to sink or swim" and it is to encourage individuals to become persons, to show individuals *how* "to swim". It is, above all, to emphasize that each individual must become a person by himself; no one can force him to do so; no one else can do it for him. There is no way of mass-producing persons. There is no "new structure" that will automatically reform and renew persons. Individuals (merely) can be "formed" by structures; persons develop chiefly from within, often against the pressures of social structures.

To become a person is to become faithful to one's own insights, and to be faithful to all the claims of one's own unrestricted drive to understand.[1] To be psychotic or neurotic is to have blocked the claims of understanding; it is to have become caught in counter-rational patterns that prevent one from acting

[1] Cf. Bernard J. F. Lonergan, S.J., *Insight: A Study of Human Understanding* (London and New York: 1957, 2nd ed. 1958).

according to all the claims of the situation in which one finds oneself. Perhaps analogously, to sin is to "turn against the light"; sin is the deliberate choice of what does not make sense, but is desired anyway. The root of a man's thirst for God is his fidelity to understanding: for, though they are not commensurate, the human activity of understanding is a participation in the life of the unseen, unknown God. To follow the claims of understanding with integrity and fidelity is to be on the path toward God. When St. Augustine sought everywhere for God, he found him not outside but within.

The ordinary structures of Catholic life in our time do not seem to show sufficient confidence in the human person. Unity is preferred to differentiation. Attention to the abstract statement is preferred to attention to the different ways in which concrete individuals understand and appropriate that statement. Community of sentiment is more cherished than a community of respect for each other's differences. In short, community is sought on too shallow a level. Confidence is lacking in the ability of men to differ profoundly and yet to be at one in respect for each other's fidelity to understanding.

There is in this matter a gap between the rhetoric of Catholics and the actual facts, between ecclesiastical structure and concrete fact. Pius XII and John XXIII were both Catholics—consecutive popes even—but such different personifications of the faith! Charles DeGaulle, Brendan Behan and Graham Greene are all Catholics: but such diversity of understanding, ideal and action! A centralized Roman structure, a comparatively uniform liturgy, a predilection for non-historical and abstract formulations of the creed, and a lack of organs of honest speech and plainly apparent differences within the Church have masked this rich diversity from the world and from Catholics themselves.

For such reasons, "ecclesiastical" has become a petty term, and even "Catholic" has come to mean its very opposite: not rich in diversity but more narrow and constricted than any moral force except communism. Many laymen in the world (perhaps especially in Anglo-Saxon countries) do not wish to be drawn within the orbit of this narrowness; they do not wish to get caught up in "Catholic" movements or be identified with "Catholic" causes. Attempts to restore Catholic community—even through the liturgy—do not appeal to all of them. It would be a mistake to think that their resistance is due only to a residue of misguided individualism. They are suspicious of new forms of ecclesiastical uniformity. They wish to be Catholic, but not ecclesiastical. They wish to retain their own personal response to faith and the integrity of their position in the secular world.

As Simone Weil once wrote, it is a mistake to think that God is interested only in religion. Likewise, it is a mistake to identify the Church with ecclesiastical structures: with the Vatican, with dioceses, with parishes. The Church is the consciousness of the Son of God—insight and love—taking root in the consciousnesses of men, sacramentally and otherwise. Because he is infinite, their diversity and number do not exhaust his life. Because each of them is finite, they cannot know him without their diversity—without each other. Their fundamental community does not arise from adherence to external structures, however important such structures be for incarnate men. Their fundamental community lies in his conscious life: he is the center toward whom they are all diversely drawn. When each man is most faithful to himself, most faithful to the unique faith which is in him, he is a source of harmony and assistance to the community. When he is unfaithful to himself, the community is deprived of his contribution.

The traditional structures of the Church that have been handed down to us do not, however, take advantage of the gifts given each individual. There do not exist forums of dialogue and communication among those who share the faith. Each of us learns so little from the other. Only the priest speaks, and he often speaks not from his own gifts but with formulae that may or may not be appropriate. It is as though we had contrived structures that could seal up all entrances against the Spirit. It is as though we had hoped that if we succeeded in fixing upon abstract formulae equally distant from all, no one of us might have the terror of encountering God face-to-face.

But if we are to propose new structures that will not keep us both from the world and from God—and that is what old ecclesiastical structures appear to do now—we must confine ourselves to concrete conditions of only one time and place. Perhaps it will be permissible, then, to discuss the situation in the United States.

Although few of our clergy or laymen speak of it, some of us are convinced that young people in the United States are undergoing a profound crisis of faith. This crisis is often hidden from sight because of a peculiarly American phenomenon. In Latin countries, at least, although many persons unquestioningly believe in God, they nevertheless do not often go to church; in the United States, on the contrary, it seems customary for many persons who are not sure whether they believe in God, or what he is like, nevertheless to go faithfully to church. It is "un-American" not to go to church.

Moreover, nearly one-half of American Catholic children and young people are in Catholic schools—some of them for all the years of their education, from grammar school through university. They early learn the habit of "frequent attendance" at the sacraments. But the early national Catholic communities are breaking up: the Irish no longer all live together, and the Slav, German and Italian sections of the big cities are beginning to yield to newer immigrant groups. In education and in occupation, American Catholics are increasingly entering into the wider American environment. It is precisely at this point that many young Catholics are beginning to doubt their faith and their own identity.

Most often they have learned their faith "by the book". Intellectually, they have lived in sheltered environments. Their faith has most often been supported by the faith of the community into which they were born. Now that in this generation large numbers of them are moving out of their native communities—many of them physically, others only spiritually—the cultural props of their faith are being left behind. The first impulse of those concerned with this situation is to create *new* Catholic communities—Newman clubs on the state university campuses, Catholic societies for lawyers, the Catholic Sociological Society, etc. Increasingly, such props appear to be artificial. Can't Catholics simply be human beings? Can't they simply take their place in the secular world? (John F. Kennedy represented an increasingly encountered type of the non-ecclesiastical, non-ghetto Catholic; he did not, for example, attend Catholic schools.)

Many young Catholics find it possible to suppress their doubts. They continue to go through the motions of belief for a long time. Such metaphysical casualness may seem strange to Europeans, but it is an important trait of the American character. In Europe there seems to be much more insistence on theoretical rigor. Every action appears to have an elaborate justification. One must be wholly convinced of the importance of *l'équipe* and "the community"; one must also be wholly committed to one's own well-developed personal creed. The American insists neither on so much "community" nor on so much "individuality". In a certain sense, the American neither *gives* so much of himself to the team, nor does he *hold back* so much of himself for a personal creed. He seems more "easygoing", less "rigid"—in a word, more "free", if also more colorless—than his European confrere. Metaphysically the American lives, to a great extent, in suspension. The demands which his many roles in society make on him and the vast range of choices open to him require him to maintain great personal flexibility.

Integrity, however, sooner or later draws its line. A choice must be made. The young American Catholic finds little in his background to prepare him for this confusion and sudden loneliness. Moreover, the moral and human development of the many nonbelievers he meets often strikes him as superior to the moral and human level of his sheltered Catholic environment. The American atheist does not seem to show the restlessness of the European atheist; atheism (or agnosticism) seems very much the sensible and admirable way of life. Many of the most intelligent young people are choosing that way, with their first real moral choice.

Not only in the United States but almost everywhere else in the world it seems increasingly that the crisis of belief and unbelief is the fundamental Christian problem of our time. It is a matter of common experience that a calm agnosticism is an attractive, admirable, livable way of life. There are two ways in which the old structures of ecclesiastical life make the agnostic choice more credible:

1. The ordinary pattern of Catholic life has too little place for open and public honesty, criticism and questioning; a sacrosanct ecclesiastical sphere has been erected in which the probing intelligence of the layman—none too delicate or gracious, perhaps—does not appear to be welcome. The ecclesiastical sphere seems a milieu of falsehood and unreality.

2. On the personal level, the old structures of Catholic preaching and practice pay too little attention to the individual's unrestricted drive to understand, that drive to destroy all false idols and to be content only with the living God. It is assumed too easily that the individual truly has appropriated his faith; belief is taken for granted, and the ways of unbelief are not cherished. But early belief is almost always belief in an idol, and the ways of unbelief are often the purifying ways to God.

These are daily realities which "new structures" in the Church must take into account. The faith of the Catholic of today cannot be supported by the props of a Catholic cultural community. To a great extent we must embrace "the Protestant principle":

reliance on the fidelity of the individual conscience, assisted by the Holy Spirit, for the ability of Catholics to take their due places in the secular world. We must develop means of discussion and consensus within the Catholic body, perhaps in the service of worship, after the example of the Quakers and the other Free Churches. Through some such voluntary associations, we must obtain the witness of diverse insight in the one community. We must teach our young people to emulate the honesty and fidelity of "the secular saints"; for to believe is to be only one step more honest, one step more faithful than they, by seeing that the momentum of honesty we feel in our hearts is the attraction of God's life within us.

PART II

BIBLIOGRAPHICAL
SURVEY

RUDOLPH SCHNACKENBURG

Born in Kattowitz, Poland, January 5, 1914. He studied at the universities of Breslau and Munich, and was ordained at Breslau on August 1, 1937. He earned his doctorate in theology in 1946 with the thesis, "Das Heilsgeschehen bei der Taufe nach dem Apostel Paulus". He taught at Dillingen/Donau and Bamberg before coming to his present post at Würzburg, where he has been a professor since 1957. He has been a consultor of the Biblical Commission since 1962. He has written many articles and a number of books on biblical subjects: *Die Johannesbriefe* (1953); *Die sittliche Botschaft des N.T.* (1954); *Gottes Herrschaft und Reich* (1959); *Die Kirche im N.T.* (1961); *La Théologie du N.T., état de la question* (1961).

JACQUES DUPONT, O.S.B.

Born December 19, 1915 in Liège, Belgium. He became a Benedictine and was ordained in 1940. He studied at the university of Louvain, the Pontifical Biblical Institute in Rome, L'Ecole Pratique des Hautes-Etudes in Paris and L'Ecole Biblique in Jerusalem. He became a master and doctor of theology, with the theses: "Sophia Theou dans les épîtres de S. Paul" (1946) and "Gnosis. La connaissance religieuse dans les épîtres de S. Paul" (1949). Since 1949 he has been professor of Sacred Scripture at the Abbey of Saint-André, Belgium. His published works include several books about the Acts of the Apostles: *Les problèmes du Livre des Actes d'après travaux récents* (1950); *Les sources du Livre des Acts* (1960); *Le discours de Milet* (1962); about christological problems: *Essais sur la Christologie de S. Jean* (1951); *Syn Christoi. L'union avec le Christ suivant S. Paul* (1952); and *Sur les Beatitudes* (1958).

Rudolph Schnackenburg/*Würzburg, W. Germany*
Jacques Dupont, O.S.B./*Bruges, Belgium*

The Church as the People of God

I

THE PEOPLE OF GOD OR THE BODY OF CHRIST?

The concept of the People of God has played a greater role in the Fathers of the Church than was once thought.[1] It is a familiar concept in the liturgy,[2] and has been brought more sharply into focus by Catholic theologians in recent years. It should not then be surprising if there has been discussion on whether or not this notion should be given a larger place in the study of ecclesiology.

It was probably with good reason, however, that the efforts of the Dominican writer, M. D. Koster, met with widespread op-

---

[1] Cf. J. Eger, *Salus Gentium. Eine patristische Studie zur Volkstheologie des Ambrosius von Mailand* (Dissertation, Munich, 1947); J. Ratzinger, *Volk und Haus Gottes in Augustins Lehre von der Kirche* (Munich, 1954); M. Schmaus, *Katholische Dogmatik,* Vol. III[1] (Munich, ed. 3-5, 1958), pp. 219-31.

[2] See the sources in Schmaus, *op. cit.,* pp. 205-11; and cf. B. Schaut, "Die Kirche als Volk Gottes: Selbstaussagen der Kirche im römischen Messbuch," in *Benedikt. Monatsschrift* 25 (1949), pp. 187-96.

position in view of the fact that he considered the concept of the People of God as the "sole, abstract, and clear designation of the Church".[3]

Until recently the Pauline concept of the Body of Christ adopted by the encyclical *Mystici Corporis Christi* was developed in the direction now familiar. Thus the feeling against the idea of the Church as the People of God persisted for some time,[4] though it was attracting more and more adherents with the theologian I. Backes of Trier as one of its advocates.[5] The increasing body of literature clearly shows that this idea is coming to the fore and is being carried to a wider audience. Apparently the Church recognizes itself in this ancient biblical concept and through it comes to a new insight into its own nature.

New studies have made it clear that the notions of the People of God and the Mystical Body of Christ complement each other in a necessary and most appropriate way. The idea of the People of God is closely connected with "God's Assembly" (*ekklesia toû theoû*), that is, the people of Israel assembled before the Lord in the Old Law, the chosen people of the covenant. In the new Dispensation, however, this people, now removed from the old association by blood and race, is newly established by the blood of Christ. It now becomes the eschatological, universal People of God composed of all the nations of the world.

This People is more accurately designated, however, as the Body of Christ, in order to reveal the fact of its reconstitution by Christ and its essential connection with Jesus as its origin, its source of life and unity, and its Savior ("Head"). This notion, too, serves to define more clearly its limits (for baptism is the

---

[3] M. D. Koster, *Ekklesiologie im Werden* (Paderborn, 1940), p. 143.

[4] See the discussion in U. Valeske, *Votum ecclesiae* (Munich, 1962), pp. 201-9, 237-50, with the rich sources and bibliography cited.

[5] "Die Kirche ist das Volk Gottes im Neuen Bund," in *Trierer theolog. Zeitschrift* 69 (1960), pp. 111-17, and "Gottesvolk im Neuen Bund," *ibid.* 70 (1961), pp. 80-93. See also under note 15 below.

act by which new members are adopted and incorporated—1 Cor. 12, 13), and to offer a clearer concept of its vital principle (the Holy Spirit: cf. 1 Cor. 3, 16; 12, 13; Eph. 2, 18.22; 4, 4), and the source of its unity and essential mark, namely, love, as manifested in the eucharistic liturgy (cf. 1 Cor. 10, 17; 11, 20-9).

On the other hand, the notion of the People of God can prevent the concept of the Mystical Body of Christ from becoming a stiff, all-too-pat model able to solve all ecclesiological problems; for example, it can offer a new, enriching dimension of the Church's continuity with the chosen people of Israel (though its distinction is clear); it can present a closer link with the Old Testament idea of a divinely ratified covenant (*diathêkê*) that finds its eschatological fulfillment in the New Law; it forms a connection with the dominant idea of Jesus' preaching, that is, of the kingdom of God (*basileia toû theoû*), and a clearer notion of the relationship between the kingdom of God and the Church; it lays stress on the eschatological and earthly-historical nature of the Church as the wandering People of God, and on the notion of God's election and man's obligation (for God's People are both holy and destined for holiness); and it implies the notion that even those who do not hold office (the laity) enjoy full membership, and suggests the contact and spread of God's People to all the nations of the world.

Thus, the idea of the People of God appears as the more embracing concept, the Mystical Body of Christ as the narrower one, in accordance with a definition suggested by Father M. Schmaus:[6] "The Church is the People of God of the New Testament, founded by Jesus Christ, hierarchically constituted for the salvation of men and the spread of God's dominion, and existing as the Mystical Body of Christ."

The exegetical foundations of this concept had already been

[6] Schmaus, *op. cit.*, p. 48.

put forward by L. Cerfaux in his monograph on the theology of the Church according to St. Paul. Here he took the concept of the People of God as the point of departure for his discussion of particular expressions and images connected with Pauline ecclesiology.[7] Since that time the idea has been further developed in scriptural,[8] dogmatic[9] and even canonical studies.[10]

II

THE CONTENT OF THE CONCEPT: THE PEOPLE OF GOD

The Norwegian scholar, N. A. Dahl, has written a monograph on the subject that embraces the Old Testament, New Testament and other Semitic literature.[11] This is a fundamental work, carefully written from the scriptural point of view with good docu-

[7] L. Cerfaux, *La théologie de l'église suivant saint Paul,* 2nd ed. (Paris, 1948); a third edition of this work is in preparation.

[8] Besides the work of Cerfaux, see also R. Schnackenburg, *Die Kirche im Neuen Testament* (Freiburg in Breisgau, 1961), pp. 133-40; P. Grelot, in *Vocabulaire de théologie biblique,* edited by X. Léon-Dufour (Paris, 1962), pp. 815-26; H. Schlier, "Zu den Namen der Kirche in den paulinischen Briefen," in *Unio christianorum: Festschrift für Erzbischof L. Jaeger* (Paderborn, 1962), pp. 147-59.
From the Protestant side, see A. Oepke, "Leib Christi oder Volk Gottes bei Paulus?", in *Theologische Literaturzeitung* 79 (1954), 363-68; P. S. Minear, *Images of the Church in the New Testament* (Philadelphia, 1960), especially chapter 3.

[9] Schmaus, *op. cit.* pp. 75-82, 211-19; I. Backes, *loc. cit.* (see note 5); J. Ratzinger, in *Lexikon für Theologie und Kirche* VI, 2nd ed. (1961), pp. 174ff.; cf. also Yves Congar, *Vraie et fausse reforme dans l'église* (Paris, 1950), pp. 133-203; Hans Küng, *Strukturen der Kirche* (Freiburg in Breisgau, 1962), pp. 19-24 (the Church as a *congregatio* and a *concilium*); Yves Congar, *Sainte Eglise* (Paris, 1963), pp. 21-44; J. Beumer, "Die Kirche: Leib Christi oder Volk Gottes?", in *Theologie und Glaube* 53 (1963), pp. 255-68.

[10] K. Mörsdorf, *Lehrbuch des Kirchenrechts* I, 7th ed. (Paderborn, 1953), pp. 20-6; A. Hagen, *Principien des kath. Kirchenrechts* (Würzburg, 1949), pp. 10f.

[11] Dahl, *Das Volk Gottes: Eine Untersuchung zum Kirchenbewusstsein des Urchristentums* (Oslo, 1941; 2nd ed. Darmstadt, 1963).

mentation and penetrating in all areas of theological discussion. Apart from a few reservations, it should be immensely profitable even to the Catholic theologian.

Another comprehensive work on *The New People of God* is by the late Protestant professor of exegesis at the University of Leipzig, A. Oepke,[12] who has followed the idea even into poetry and drama and the arts. The historical section (pp. 84-467) treats the period from Moses to Luther. Here the author investigates especially the relationship between the People of God of the Old and the New Law, between the People of God and individual nations (and, indeed, the Church and the kingdoms of the world), and goes into such questions as "revelation and God's People", "God's People and morality". The book is a mine of source material and ideas. It gives some notion of the historical influence and the broad expanse of this concept in time, although it is slightly less useful from the ecclesiological point of view.

From the Catholic side we are fortunate in having a fair number of good surveys. A typical one is P. Grelot's *Vocabulaire de théologie biblique:*[13] the People of God of the Old Testament is a religious society that God has elected and consecrated for his service; it is at the same time an earthly society, united by race, language, country, and civil laws. The people of Israel, however, sees itself as merely an imperfect expression of the divine idea, and awaits a new, universal covenant with God in the future, in which the perfect communion between God and his People will be realized. In this new Dispensation, established in the blood of Jesus, the eschatological hopes will be fulfilled, and a new People of God is formed that must then proceed to its own ultimate perfection.

These main lines of thought are again put forward by R.

---

[12] *Das neue Gottesvolk in Schrifttum, bildender Kunst und Weltgestaltung* (Gütersloh, 1950).

[13] *Loc. cit.*, see note 8.

Schnackenburg with particular emphasis on the New Testament.[14] In a collection that brings together articles by Catholic and Lutheran authors, H. Gross discusses "The People of God in the Old Testament", and I. Backes "The People of God in the New Testament".[15] And there are articles by J. Scharbert and V. Warnach in the *Bibeltheologisches Wörterbuch*.[16]

The Old Testament

There are more specialized works on the Old Testament by Catholic scholars. An extensive discussion in Spanish[17] by P. Asensio, S.J., is especially commendable for its chapters on Yahweh's presence in Israel (pp. 109-60), and on the promise, "I will be your God and you will be my people" (pp. 204-38), with reference to the messianic period of the New Law.

For a treatment of the basic ideas of divine election, the covenant, and the chosen people in the Deuteronomic code, the fundamental study of G. von Rad appeared some time ago.[18] There is a shorter study of the idea on the whole of the Old Testament by H. J. Kraus.[19] And we have a monograph on the important text, Exodus 19, 30-8, by H. Wildberger, who discusses the historical tradition of this proclamation of Israel as God's chosen people.[20] While Wildberger tends to put forward some extreme hypotheses, the concept of Yahweh's priestly and royal kingdom, his "holy People", and the idea of divine election

---

[14] *Loc. cit.*, see note 8.

[15] H. Asmussen, I. Backes, and others, *Die Kirche: Volk Gottes* (Stuttgart, 1961); see especially H. Gross, "Volk Gottes im Alten Testament," pp. 67-96, and I. Backes, "Das Volk Gottes im Neuen Testament," pp. 97-129.

[16] V. Warnach, "Kirche," *Bibeltheologisches Wörterbuch*, 2nd ed., J. B. Bauer, ed. (Graz, 1962), pp. 693-717; J. Scharbert, "Volk (Gottes)," *ibid.*, pp. 1147-58.

[17] *Yahveh y su pueblo*, in *Analecta Gregoriana* 58 (Rome, 1953).

[18] *Das Volk Gottes im Deuteronomium* (Stuttgart, 1929).

[19] *Das Volk Gottes im Alten Testament* (Zurich, 1938).

[20] H. Wildberger, *Jahwes Eigentumsvolk* (Zurich, 1960).

are clearly brought out (pp. 74-117). Indeed, Exodus 19, 5-6, which has exercised a wide influence down to New Testament times (cf. Titus 2, 14; 1 Peter 2, 9; and Apoc. 1, 6; 5, 10), has been examined by exegetes with rather different conclusions.[21] Among the relevant studies on the Old Testament are those on the concept of election, on which there exists a considerable number of monographs.[22]

The New Testament

Within different contexts there are a good number of treatments of the People of God in the New Testament, either touching on the special problem of the relationship of Israel with the Church (see under note 3 above), or discussing the idea as it emerges in individual New Testament writers (see under note 4). A book in English by D. G. Miller,[23] intended for a more popular audience, manifests a general concern for the notion and role of the Church, without, however, developing the aspect of the People of God. L. Newbigin puts forward the interesting view[24] that the idea of the People of God favors a more Protestant type of ecclesiology, the Mystical Body a more Catholic one, while the concept of the temple of the Holy Spirit lends itself to the illuminationist sects of the pentecostal variety. But

[21] Cf. J. Bauer, "Konige und Priester, ein heiliges Volk (Ex. 19, 6)," in *Bibl. Zeitschrift* 2 (1958), pp. 283-6; W. L. Moran, "A Kingdom of Priests," in *The Bible in Current Catholic Thought*, J. L. McKenzie, ed. (1962), pp. 7-20; G. Fohrer, "Priesterliches Königtum; Ex. 19, 6," in *Theolog. Zeitschrift* 19 (1961), pp. 359-62.

[22] H. H. Rowley, *The Biblical Doctrine of Election* (London, 1950); T. C. Vriezen, *Die Erwählung Israels nach dem Alten Testament* (Zurich, 1953); B. W. Helfgott, *The Doctrine of Election in Tannaitic Literature* (New York and London, 1955); C. Schedl, "Bund und Erwählung," in *Zeitschrift für kath. Theologie* 80 (1958), pp. 493-515. On J. Jocz see note 33 below.

[23] *The People of God*, (London, 1959).

[24] *L'Église, peuple des croyants, Corps du Christ, Temple de l'Esprit* (Paris, 1958).

surely these are questionable categories tending to an over-simplification, seeing that he would assign to different Churches and sects concepts which our knowledge of the Bible and of the primitive Christian tradition should urge us to consider together.

III

THE RELATIONSHIP BETWEEN THE ANCIENT CHOSEN PEOPLE OF GOD AND THE NEW PEOPLE OF GOD, THE CHURCH

Much has been written on this subject with reference to the theological point of view as well as to the historical confrontation between Israel and the Church. We should, however, keep these two questions clearly apart, even though there are connections between theological and historical approaches. Here, however, we must exclude the second aspect of the problem, which has indeed been beset with a centuries-old history of guilt and suffering. We must confine ourselves to the theological aspect of the problem, and, in particular, the thorny problem of the relationship between the Church and Israel in the New Testament, a question of enormous importance for ecclesiology. This problem has been discussed in both of the great studies mentioned earlier, and is duly noticed in the relevant articles in Kittel's *Theologisches Worterbuch zum Neuen Testament*,[25] and has been discussed as well in a number of specialized works.

The difficulty consists in the conflict already recognizable in the New Testament. On the one hand, the People of God of the New Law are the legitimate continuation, the messianic fulfillment of the chosen people of the Old Testament, and hence they stand in the direct line of succession as the true Israel in the

---

[25] See W. Gutbrod, *TWNT* III, pp. 386-91, H. Strathmann, IV, pp. 53-7. On the expression "the Israel of God" in Galatians 6, 16, see the discussion of the controversy in Schnackenburg, *Die Kirche im Neuen Testament*, p. 73.

divine scheme. On the other hand, they are a new creation on the basis of Christ's atonement (the *new* Israel); and hence there is a distinct break in the continuity inasmuch as the old Israel by its rejection of Jesus as the Messiah is no longer part of the new community.

Neither of these aspects should be neglected, appearing as they do with varying degrees of emphasis in St. Paul and the other New Testament writers. And if the expression, "the new Israel", does not appear in the New Testament,[26] this is all the more reason for holding fast to the notion that God has not revoked his promises to Israel, and that the Church of the Gentiles has merely been grafted onto his chosen people, and it is the complete and total Israel that is to be saved in the end (Rom. 9-11).[27] At the same time we cannot deny the fact that the Church, constituted as the People of God in the blood of Jesus (Eph. 2, 11-22), is a new entity, chosen from all peoples, Gentile and Jew.

Our view of this non-Christian Israel has been vitiated by many false or questionable discussions of the problem. The attempt to correct such erroneous interpretations, which have filtered even into classroom textbooks, is all the more to be welcomed.[28] In the first place there should be no question of a

---

[26] See M. Carrez, "Le nouvel Israël. Réflexions sur l'absence de cette désignation de l'Église dans le Nouveau Testament," *Foi et Vie* 6 (1959), pp. 30-4.

[27] See F. W. Maier, *Israel in der Heilsgeschichte nach Röm. 9-11* (Münster i. W., 1929); E. Peterson, *Die Kirche aus Juden und Heiden* (Salzburg); K. L. Schmidt, *Die Judenfrage im Lichte der Kapitel 9-11 des Römerbriefes,* 2nd ed. (Zurich, 1947); G. Schrenk, *Die Weissagung über Israel im Neuen Testament* (Zurich, 1951); J. Munck, *Christus und Israel. Eine Auslegung von Röm. 9-11* (Copenhagen, 1956); see also three articles in "Studiorum Paulinorum Congressus Internationalis Catholicus 1961," in *Analecta Biblica* 17-18 (Rome, 1963) vol. I, pp. 309-15 by X. Léon-Dufour, pp. 317-27 by J. M. Osterreicher, and pp. 329-40 by F. J. Caubet Iturbe.

[28] See J. Isaac, *Jesus et Israel* (Paris, 1948); P. Démann, *La catéchèse chrétienne et le peuple de la Bible* (Paris, 1952).

definitive rejection of Israel;[29] at the same time it is clear from Matthew's Gospel that the Israelites who reject Jesus are not to be numbered among the New People of God.[30]

The difficulty with any far-reaching generalization is demonstrated by D. Judant,[31] whose book on the two Israels is open to some criticism despite a sound structure; and similarly by the theological discussion of K. Thiemes,[32] who would grant all Jews of goodwill even further privileges in virtue of their ancient calling, and consider them as the elder brother of the parable of the Prodigal Son (Luke 15).

On the Anglican side there has appeared a notable treatment of the theology of election by the Jewish convert J. Jocz.[33] In his chapter on the Jews and the Church (pp. 95-126) the difficulties are in any case brought to the fore. This question surely calls for more extensive theological investigation.

IV. SPECIAL TEXTS AND PARTICULAR ASPECTS OF THE PROBLEM

Especially valuable are works that treat individual texts of importance for the general idea or handle otherwise neglected aspects of the question. Of significance, first of all, is the speech of James at the Council of Jerusalem in the Acts of the Apostles 15, 14: "Simeon hath declared how God at the first did visit the Gentiles, to take out of them a people (*laos*) for his name." For this is evidence for the divine invitation of the Gentiles to be-

[29] Cf. A. Lacoque, "Israel, pierre de touche de l'oecuménisme," in *Verbum Caro* 12 (1958), pp. 331-43; F. Lousky, "Remarques sur la notion de rejet par rapport au mystère d'Israël et l'unité de l'Église," in *Rev. d'histoire et de philosophie relig.* 43 (1963), pp. 32-47.

[30] W. Trilling, *Das wahre Israel. Studien zur Theologie des Matthäusevangeliums* (Leipzig, 1959); R. Hummel, *Die Auseinandersetzung zwischen Kirche und Judentum im Matthäusevangelium* (Munich, 1963).

[31] *Les Deux Israël* (Paris, 1960), and see the review by R. Benoit in *Revue biblique* 68 (1961), pp. 458-62.

[32] "Das Mysterium der Kirche in der christlichen Sicht des alten Bundesvolk," in *Mysterium Kirche in der Sicht der theologischen Disziplinen*, Vol. I, F. Holböck and T. Sartory, eds. (Salzburg, 1962), pp. 37-88.

[33] J. Jocz, *A Theology of Election: Israel and the Church* (London, 1958).

come the People of God, and an early witness (probably based on Zachariah 2, 15) for the primitive Church's awareness of its own nature.[34]

The most rewarding text, however, from a theological point of view is Acts 20, 28. For here we have in a nutshell all the New Testament theology of the People of God: the assembly of God (*ekklesia toû theoû*) is also God's chosen People (cf. Ps. 74, 2), which God has newly purchased by the blood of his Son; and, under another image, it is the flock over which the Holy Spirit has placed "overseers".[35]

It is clear here that the concept of the People of God also implies direction by shepherds appointed by God. It is gratifying that this departure speech of St. Paul—or, rather, his spiritual testament—has been attracting greater attention among scholars.[36]

The same cannot be said of the classic text, 1 Peter 2, 9-10. It is usually discussed in connection with the general priesthood of the laity,[37] but deserves a more penetrating investigation from the ecclesiological point of view; for in connection with the idea of the "spiritual house" (1 Peter 2, 5), which is linked with the concept of the Mystical Body through Ephesians 2, 20ff., this text can become a rich addition to our understanding of the Church's nature.

[34] Cf. J. Dupont, "*Laos ex ethnôn* (Acts XV, 14)," in *New Testament Studies* 3 (1956-57), pp. 47-50; N. A. Dahl, "A People for His Name (Acts XV, 14)," in *New Testament Studies* 3 (1956-7), pp. 319-27.

[35] See R. Schnackenburg, "Episkopos und Hirtenamt," in *Episcopos* (*Festschrift Faulhaber*) (Regensburg, 1949), pp. 66-88.

[36] J. Dupont, *Le discours de Milet, testament pastoral de saint Paul* (Paris, 1962), especially pp. 167-73; H. Schürmann, "Das Testament des Paulus für die Kirche, Apg. 20, 18-35," in *Unio christianorum: Festschrift für Erzbischof L. Jaeger* (Paderborn, 1962) pp. 108-46.

[37] Cf. P. Ketter, "Das allgemeine Priestertum der Gläubigen nach dem 1. Petrusbrief," in *Trierer theol. Zeitschrift* 56 (1947), pp. 43-51; J. Blinzler, "Hierateuma," in *Episcopus*, pp. 49-65; L. Cerfaux, "Regale Sacerdotium," in *Receuil L. Cerfaux* II (Gembloux, 1954), pp. 283-315; Yves Congar, *Jalons pour une théologie du laïcat* (Paris, 1953).

We are only beginning to discover the rich treasures of the epistle to the Hebrews for the idea of the People of God. Here the wandering people of the Old Testament crossing the desert to the Promised Land becomes the type of the eschatological People of the New Law, who already experience the fulfillment of the promise, yet are still on the way to perfection and require divine protection (Heb. 3, 7-4.11).[38] It is surprising that this idea has not, so far as we can learn, been more widely taken up on a popular level.

In this connection, the riches of the Apocalypse have not yet been fully exploited. Here we have a rather central image of God's community under the symbol of the heavenly Woman (Apoc. 12); the people divided into twelve tribes and it is from them that the Messiah emerges; the messianic community in persecution and miraculously delivered.[39]

Until now the discussion of these texts has been largely devoted to Mariological questions. J. Comblin has given us a very striking and impressive exegesis of the section used for the epistle of the Mass for All Saints Day (Apoc. 7, 2-12):[40] here the Church is considered as the community of the elect, marked with the seal of Christ; it is the eschatological Israel, raised to cosmic dimensions. It is a liturgical community made up of all the peoples and nations of the world, actually on earth and yet linked with the assemblage in heaven, an anticipation of the

[38] See A. Oepke, *loc. cit.*, pp. 17-24, 57-74; F. J. Schierse, *Verheissung und Heilsvollendung. Zur theologischen Grundfrage des Hebräerbriefes* (Munich, 1955); R. Schnackenburg, *Die Kirche im Neuen Testament*, pp. 81-86.

[39] Apart from the commentaries on the passage, see especially B. J. Le Trois, *The Woman Clothed with the Sun* (Rome, 1954); A. T. Kassing, *Die Kirche und Maria, Ihr Verhältnis im 12. Kap. der Apokalypse* (Düsseldorff, 1958); J. Michl, "Die deutung der apokalyptischen Frau in der Gegenwart," in *Bibl. Zeitschrift* 3 (1959), pp. 301-10, with the literature cited.

[40] See J. Comblin, "Le ressemblement de l'Israël de Dieu (Apoc. 7, 2-12)," in *Fête de la Toussaint* (*Assemblées du Seigneur* 89, Bruges, 1963), pp. 15-33.

glorious People of the heavenly Jerusalem. Here, indeed, is the fruit of biblical study that has been focussed on the eschatological history of salvation. We can only hope that it will be more and more incorporated into ecclesiological thought.

BONIFACE WILLEMS, O.P.

Born in Rotterdam, Holland, December 4, 1926.
He studied philosophy and theology with the Do-
minicans at Zwolle and Nijmegen, and was ordained in 1952. Further studies followed at the
universities of Münster, Basle and Straatsburg. He
earned his doctorate in 1957 at Münster with the
thesis, "Kirchenzugehörigkeit als Heilsnotwendigkeit". At present he is professor of dogmatic theology at the Albertinum in Nijmegen. His theological interests are shown in many articles about
the Church, as well as in his writings about such
personalities as Karl Barth and Karl Jaspers: cf.
his book *Karl Barth* (1963), and the collective
work *Mens en God* (1963).

Boniface Willems, O.P./*Nijmegen, Netherlands*

Who Belongs to the Church?

This survey concerns the necessity of the Church for salvation and the associated problem of the Church's boundaries. Recent years have shown an increasing urgency and a wider perspective in the treatment of this problem. Since Yves Congar's pioneering work, *Chrétiens désunis* (Paris, 1937), and Pius XII's great encyclical *Mystici Corporis Christi* of 1943, a vast literature has appeared dealing with these issues of the Church's membership and its boundaries.

Many of these studies sprang from ecumenical preoccupations. Taking for granted that the Church is necessary for salvation, authors examined the question whether and, if so, how non-Catholic Christians nevertheless belong to the Church of Christ. Both the accelerating tempo of the movement toward world unity that forced Christianity to take stock of itself in the present situation, and the very dynamics of a doctrine that maintained the necessity of the Church for salvation, gradually brought the question to the fore in missiology and in other scientific approaches to religion as well.[1] For these various reasons there developed greater sympathy for the problems raised by those who, while living in a society based on Christian culture, reject the Christian claim to exclusiveness.[2]

This widening of the context brought about certain changes in the formulation of the problem. If, initially, it was still possible to use every kind of theological acumen to point to the salutary influence of the Church on the individual outsider, authors began to examine the question of the possible significance of non-Catholic Christian religions in the economy of salvation, as Congar had already done in 1937. Subsequently, the same question was also raised in connection with non-Christian religions.

Extra Ecclesiam Nulla Salus

It is not possible to trace, step by step, the development outlined above as the stages sometimes overlap chronologically. For practical purposes this survey is limited to publications that appeared after 1950, and among these almost exclusively to those by Catholic authors.[3]

Every theological problem provokes a definite historical investigation.[4] Thus the re-examination of the adage *extra eccle-*

[1] E. Loffeld, *Le problème cardinal de la missiologie et des missions catholiques* (Rhenen, 1956); A. Santos Hernandez, *Salvación y Paganismo. El Problema teológico de la salvación de los infieles* (Santander, 1960); H. R. Schlette, *Die Religionen als Thema der Theologie* (Freiburg, 1963); *The Theology of the Christian Mission*, G. H. Anderson, ed. (*World Missionary Studies*, London, 1961).

[2] See *inter alia* J. Huxley, *Religion without Revelation* (Mentor Books, 1957); K. Jaspers, *Der philosophische Glaube angesichts der Offenbarung* (Munich, 1962); F. Jeanson, *La foi d'un incroyant* (Paris, 1963); G. Szczesny, *Die Zukunft des Unglaubens* (Munich, 1958).

[3] The most recent Protestant studies on this subject, with extensive bibliographical notes, are: W. Dietzfelbinger, *Die Grenzen der Kirche nach römisch-katholischer Lehre* (Göttingen, 1962); U. Valeske, *Votum Ecclesiae* (Munich, 1962).

[4] P. Soullard, "Les infidèles peuvent-ils être sauvés? Etapes historiques de la question," in *Lumière et Vie* 18 (1954), pp. 51-72; L. Capéran, *L'Appel des non-chrétiens au salut* (Paris, 1961).

siam nulla salus (outside the Church there is no salvation) naturally led to an investigation into the original meaning of this phrase. A. Seitz had already published an extensive study on this question in 1903.[5]

Since then it has become evident, on the one hand, that Cyprian's taut formula stood in a context hardly orthodox, and, on the other hand, that Cyprian spoke under the impression that Christ's Second Coming was imminent. The usual context of Cyprian's formula is the quarrel over the validity of sacraments outside the Church. Cyprian held, against Rome, that baptism by a heretic was invalid. He justified his position by declaring that "there is no salvation outside the Church". How, then, could baptism outside the Church be valid? In spite of the formula, however, there lies something positive behind Cyprian's uncompromising exclusivism.

God granted the world salvation in Christ. Christ confirmed this salvation by founding a Church community. The unity and communion of the Church, gathered round the bishop, *is* salvation because this community of Christians is precisely the communion of and with the Father, the Son and the Holy Spirit. Outside this unity, of which the integral faith, the *fides integra,* is an essential part, the Antichrist sows division and therefore perdition, and this betokens the imminent end of the world.[6]

To achieve clear understanding a dogmatic formula needs, apart from the correct reconstruction of its historical origin, the study of its scriptural basis and the teaching of the magisterium. Insofar as the scriptural basis is concerned most studies used to be somewhat restricted. They pointed to the clear teaching of Scripture on the necessity of faith and baptism on the one hand,

[5] A. Seitz, *Die Heilsnotwendigkeit der Kirche nach der altchristlichen Literatur bis zur Zeit des Hl. Augustins* (Freiburg, 1903).

[6] R. Hardowirjono, "S. Cypriaan: Het heil in de kerk," in *Bijdragen* 19 (1958), pp. 1-21 and 137-61; G. Kopf, "Hors de l'église point de salut. Origines d'une formule équivoque," in *Cahiers univers. cath.* 6-7 (1953), pp. 302-10; Dict. *Catholicisme,* V. cc. 948-50; LThK III, 2nd ed., cc. 1320-1321.

and on the other hand, to the universality of God's saving will.[7] The condemnation of non-Jews and non-Christians in the Bible, however, usually refers to those who have consciously rejected God's call. Within the scriptural framework there is room for "saintly Gentiles".[8] St. Paul, too, teaches that, though salvation is never bestowed independently of the Church, non-baptized persons can, nevertheless, in a mysterious way share in Christ's redemption.[9]

It has also been pointed out that Scripture recognizes a kind of "anonymous" belonging to Christ. In Matthew 25, 34-40, the king says to those at his right hand, "Come, blessed of my Father, take possession of the kingdom prepared for you from the foundation of the world; for I was hungry and you gave me to eat," etc. The significant reaction of the elect is, "Lord, when did we see thee hungry?" They cannot remember ever having met Christ. Upon which the king says, "Truly, I say to you, as you did it for one of the least of these my brethren, you did it for me."

There exists, therefore, an encounter with Christ that is not explicitly conscious, and that takes place in the encounter with one's neighbor.[10] In support of this "implicit" Christianity, scholars also quote St. Paul's discourse on the Areopagus, "What therefore you worship as unknown, this I proclaim to you" (Acts 17, 23).[11]

[7] C. García Extremeño, "La necesidad de la iglesia para salvarse," in *Studium* 2 (1962), esp. pp. 34-38; A. Santos Hernandez, *Salvación y Paganismo* (Santander, 1960), pp. 186-87, 215-17 and 402; R. Lombardi, *La salvezza di chi non ha fede,* 4th ed. (Rome, 1949); H. R. Schlette, *op. cit.,* pp. 24, 34-8, 75-80.

[8] J. Daniélou, *Les saints païens et l'Ancien Testament* (Paris, 1956).

[9] J. M. Gonzalez Ruiz, " 'Extra ecclesiam nulla salus' a la luz de la teología paulina," in *Estud. Bibl.* 19 (1960), pp. 25-48.

[10] Yves Congar, "Au sujet des non-catholiques," in *Rev. des Sc. Rel.* 3 (1958), pp. 53-65, also in *Sainte Eglise* (Paris, 1963), pp. 433-44, English tr. in *Blackfriars* (1957), pp. 290-300; *id., Ausser der Kirche kein Heil* (Essen, 1961); J. Ratzinger, *Die christliche Brüderlichkeit* (Munich, 1960).

[11] A. Röper, *Die anonymen Christen* (Mainz, 1963).

The attitude of the magisterium on the point of the Church's necessity for salvation has been more extensively examined by many scholars.[12] This necessity was explicitly taught by Innocent III (Denz. 423), the fourth Lateran Council (Denz. 430), Boniface VIII in his bull *Unam Sanctam* (Denz. 468-469) and Clement VI (Denz. 570b). The Council of Florence, under Eugene IV (Denz. 714), even adopted a harsh statement by Fulgentius of Ruspe: "Neither pagans nor Jews, heretics and schismatics can obtain eternal life but will be condemned to the everlasting fire which is prepared for the devil and his angels unless, before the end of their lives, they are received into the Catholic Church." This text of Fulgentius, however, owed its great traditional authority to the false supposition that it came from St. Augustine.[13]

Since Pius IX the arguments used against indifferentism are no longer limited to the necessity of the Church but include a more positive reference to the possible salvation of those who live in invincible ignorance of the Christian religion (Denz. 1647, 1677). This reference is constantly mentioned by Leo XIII (*A.S.S.* XXVIII, 1895-1896, p. 708) and Pius X (*A.A.S.* XXXVI, 1903-1904, p. 136 and *A.A.S.* III, 1911, p. 564). The preparatory documents for the unpublished second constitution on the Church for the first Vatican Council also referred to the possibility of an invincible ignorance of the Church (*Mansi* 51, 541). There were moreover objections to the distinction between belonging to the Church *re* (in actual fact) and *voto* (in wish), just as there were objections to the distinction between

[12] L. Capéran, *op. cit.;* Yves Congar, "Hors de l'Eglise pas de salut," in *Sainte Eglise* (Paris, 1963), pp. 417-32 (= Dict. *Catholicisme* V, cc. 948-56; C. García Extremeño, *op. cit.,* pp. 6-44; K. Rahner, *Schriften zur Theologie,* Pt. 2 (Einsiedeln, 1955), pp. 7-94; F. Shea, "The Principles of Extra-Sacramental Justification in Relation to 'Extra Ecclesiam Nulla Salus'," in *Proceedings Cath. Theological Soc. of America* (1955), pp. 125-51; S. Tromp, *De Spiritu Christi Anima* (Rome, 1960), pp. 184-215.

[13] J. Beumer, "Zwischen Patristik und Scholastik," in *Gregorianum* 23 (1942), pp. 326-47.

belonging to the "soul" and to the "soul-and-body" of the Church (*Mansi* 49, 624-625, 570-571).[14]

THE ENCYCLICAL "MYSTICI CORPORIS CHRISTI"

The teaching on Church membership as propounded in the encyclical *Mystici Corporis Christi,* and reinforced by *Humani Generis* (*A.A.S.* XLII, 1950, p. 571) continued to stimulate further study, even after the many initial reactions.[15] It was found, on the one hand, that the definition of Church membership was conceived in purely juridical categories, contrary to what many great and traditional theologians like St. Thomas had written about it.[16] On the other hand, there did not seem to be any striking differences compared with earlier statements by the magisterium, apart from a clearer terminological equation of Church and the Mystical Body of Christ.

[14] J. Beumer, "Ekklesiologische Fragen auf dem Vatikanischen Konzil," in *Münch. Theol. Zeitscher* 5 (1954) pp. 236-45; *id.,* "Die Heilsnotwendigkeit der Kirche nach den Akten des Vatikanischen Konzils," in *Theol. und Glaube* 38 (1947-1948), pp. 76-86; L. Boisvert, *Doctrina de membris Ecclesiae iuxta documenta magisterii recentiora a Concilio Vaticano primo ad encyclicum Mystici Corporis* (Montreal, 1962); G. García Quintana, "El axioma 'Extra Ecclesiam nulla salus' según el esquema De Ecclesia Christi propuesto al Concilio Vaticano," in *Eccles. Xaveriana* 1 (1951), pp. 71-90; F. van der Horst, *Das Schema über die Kirche auf dem ersten vatikanischen Konzil* (Paderborn, 1963), pp. 209-56; J. King, *The Necessity of the Church for Salvation in Selected Theological Writings of the Past Century* (Washington, 1960), pp. 30-3.

[15] K. Algermissen, "Aktuelle Mitgliedschaft in der Kirche und gnadenhafte Zugehörigkeit zu ihr," in *Theol. und Glaube* 46 (1956), pp. 260-75; C. G. Extremeño, "La necesidad de la iglesia para salvarse," in *Studium* 2 (1962), esp. pp. 21-29; D. M. Nothomb, "L'Eglise et le Corps Mystique," in *Irénikon* 25 (1952), pp. 226-48; K. Rahner, *Schriften zur Theologie,* Pt. 2 (Einsiedeln, 1955), pp. 40-75; E. Sauras, "The Members of the Church," in *The Thomist* 27 (1963), pp. 78-87.

[16] C. E. O'Neill, "St. Thomas on the Membership of the Church," in *The Thomist* 27 (1963), pp. 88-140; *id.,* "Members of the Church: Mystici Corporis and St. Thomas," in *Amer. Eccl. Rev.* 148 (1963), pp. 113-28, 167-84.

According to the encyclical one cannot hold in the present phase of salvation history that somebody can be a member of the Mystical Body without being a member of the Church. There is, indeed, a distinction between actual Church membership (*in re*) and a grace-inspired turning toward the Church (*in voto*).

A letter (August 8, 1949) was sent by the Holy Office to Archbishop (now Cardinal) Cushing of Boston that is important on precisely this point.[17] In the decisive passages, this letter quotes, sometimes verbatim, an explanation given by Billot in 1919.[18] The letter was provoked by the activities of Fr. Feeney who propagated the idea, particularly among students of Harvard University, that anyone who did not become an actual member of the Church was damned.[19]

The Holy Office compared the necessity of the Church with that of baptism. Just as there is baptism of desire, so it is not always necessary *ut quis . . . reapse ecclesiae tamquam membrum incorporetur, sed id saltem requiritur ut eidem voto vel desiderio adhaereat* (that a person be actually incorporated in the Church as a member, but it is at least required that he belong to it in wish or desire). Closely following Billot, however, the letter goes further than this. The desire to belong to the Church need not be explicit as is the case with catechumens. In the case of those who live in invincible ignorance: *Deus quoque implicitum votum acceptat, tali nomine nuncupatum, quia illud in ea bona animae dispositione continetur, qua homo voluntatem suam Dei voluntati conformem velit* (God also accepts the implicit wish, so-called because it lies in that right disposition of the soul by which a man wishes his will to conform to that of

[17] First published in *Amer. Eccl. Rev.* 127 (1952), pp. 307-11; afterward in *Rev. Esp. de Teol.* 13 (1953), pp. 69-72. Cf. *Denz.* 3866-3873.

[18] L. Billot, "La providence de Dieu et le nombre infini des hommes hors de la voie normale du salut," in *Etudes* 56 (1919), esp. pp. 145-6. Cf. B. A. Willems, "De algemene heilsoorzakelijkheid van de kerk," in *Jaarboek kath. theol. in Nederland* (1962), p. 32.

[19] For an extensive narrative of this affair see Cath. Goddard Clarke, *The Loyolas and the Cabots* (Boston, 1950).

God). The further development of this theme adds that this implicit wish or desire must be imbued with perfect love (*perfecta caritate informetur*) and that it cannot save without supernatural faith (*nisi homo habeat fidem supernaturalem*), where Hebrews 11, 6 is referred to.[20]

THE "SOUL" AND THE "BODY" OF THE CHURCH

The teaching, then, on being turned toward the Church by implicit desire thus obtained a certain confirmation. This indeed follows logically from understanding what the Church is. As long as one held the dualistic view that the Church as an institution is opposed to the Church as community of grace, it was possible to maintain the distinction between belonging to the soul-and-body of the Church and belonging to the soul only. As, however, the sacramental vision of the Church outgrew the dualistic view[21] by seeing in the "institution" precisely the mani-

[20] Yves Congar, "Hors de l'Eglise pas de salut," in *Vers l'Unité chrét.* 58 (1953), pp. 3-5; J. Fenton, "The Holy Office Letter on the Necessity of the Catholic Church," in *Amer. Eccl. Rev.* 127 (1952), pp. 450-61; C. G. Extremeño, "La necesidad de la iglesia para salvarse," in *Studium* 2 (1962), esp. pp. 29-34; A. Hoffman, "Die Heilsnotwendigkeit der Kirche nach einer authentischen Erklärung des Hl. Offiziums," in *Die Neue Ordnung* 7 (1953), pp. 90-9; J. Iturrioz, "La herejía de Boston," in *Hechos y Dichos* (1953), pp. 525-32; A. Minon, "Une explication officielle de l'adage 'hors de l'Eglise pas de salut'," in *Rev. eccl. de Liège* 42 (1955), pp. 111-17; G. Montesi, "Skandal in Boston," in *Wort und Wahrheit* 6 (1951), pp. 233-6; E. K. Winter, "Extra Ecclesiam nulla salus," in *Hochland* 42 (1950), pp. 230-6; *id.*, "Häresie in Boston?" in *Schweiz. Rundschau* 49 (1949), pp. 601-8; T. Zapelena, *De Ecclesia Christi*, pars 2a, 2nd ed. (Rome, 1954), pp. 319-28.

[21] C. García Extremeño, "La necesidad de la iglesia para salvarse," in *Studium* 3 (1963), esp. pp. 73-5; M. J. Le Guillou, *Le Christ et l'Eglise* (Paris, 1963); S. Jáki, *Les tendences nouvelles de l'ecclesiologie* (Rome, 1957), p. 245; A. Lorschneider, "O Mistério da Igreja," in *Rev. Ecles. Brasil* 23 (1963), p. 881; H. de Lubac, *Méditation sur l'Eglise*, 2nd ed. (Paris, 1953), pp. 175-203; K. Rahner, *Kirche und Sakramente* (Freiburg, 1960); E. Schillebeeckx, "Sakramente als Organe der Gottbegegnung," in *Fragen der Theologie heute* (Einsiedeln, 1957), pp. 379-401; O. Semmel-

festation and earthly presence of the eschatological reality of God's grace, so also grew the awareness that whoever in any way belongs to the "soul" of the Church, must in the same way and to the same degree belong to the "body" of the Church. Bellarmine's authority made the distinction between the soul and the body of the Church popular for a long time, but the way in which he attributed this distinction to St. Augustine is historically questionable.[22]

All this helped to bring some clarity into the terminology. A distinction is made between those who are members of the Church and those who are, so to speak, orientated toward the Church. The latter are not yet members of the Church. All this is mainly a question of terminology. Many theologians wish to reserve the expression "member" of the Church strictly to those who fulfill all the conditions laid down for membership of the Church by the encyclical *Mystici Corporis Christi:* confession of the true faith, reception of the sacrament of baptism and communion with the hierarchical community.[23]

---

roth, *Die Kirche als Ursakrament* (Frankfurt, 1953); B. A. Willems, "Der sakramentale Kirchenbegriff," in *Freib. Zeitschr. Phil. und Theol.* 5 (1958), pp. 274-96. A critical contrast may be found in, *inter alia,* J. Hamer, *L'Eglise est une communion* (Paris, 1962), pp. 91-5 and Yves Congar, *La Sainte Eglise* (Paris, 1963), p. 623.

[22] J. Beumer, "Die kirchliche Gliedschaft in der Lehre des hl. Robert Bellarmin," in *Theol. und Glaube* 38 (1948), pp. 243-57; R. Brunet, "Les dissidents de bonne foi sont-ils membres de l'Eglise?" in *Anal. Greg.* 68 (1954), pp. 199-218; J. Hardon, *A Comparative Study of Bellarmine's Doctrine of the Relation of Sincere non-Catholics to the Church* (Rome, 1951); F. van der Horst, *Das Schema uber die Kirche* (Paderborn, 1963), pp. 235-6; J. Fenton, "The Meaning of the Church's Necessity for Salvation," in *Amer. Eccl. Rev.* 124 (1951), pp. 124-43, 203-21 and 290-302 suggests that the misunderstanding is due, not to Bellarmine himself, but to later authors, especially Tournely. Cf. M. Schmaus, "Die Kirchengliedschaft nach Honoré de Tournely," in *Festgabe Jos. Lortz* (Baden-Baden, 1958), pp. 447-68.

[23] K. Algermissen, *op. cit.,* pp. 260-75; R. Brunet, *op. cit.,* pp. 199-218; J. King, *op. cit.;* K. Rahner, *Schriften zur Theologie,* II (Einsiedeln, 1955), pp. 29-40; S. Tromp, *op. cit.; id.,* "De Ecclesiae Membris," in *Divinitas* 6 (1962), pp. 481-92; J. Vodopivec, "Membri in re ed ap-

There is, however, an understandable tendency to bring out the fact that baptism, validly administered, is the basis of Church membership.[24] According to the terminology as given above, both those Christians who are not in communion with Rome and those who are outside every form of Christianity can only be said to belong to the Church *in voto,* if at all. This *votum* is in any case not a purely interior factor, as we shall see. But the objective reality in which this *votum* takes shape becomes in all baptized Christians a genuine Christian reality.

Canon lawyers have, therefore, pointed to canon 87,[25] which says that baptism makes man a person in the Church of Christ with all the rights and offices of a Christian unless, insofar as the rights are concerned, there is an obstacle that breaks the bond of communion with the Church or is caused by a pronounced ecclesiastical censure (*Baptismate homo constituitur in Ecclesia Christi persona cum omnibus christianorum iuribus et officiis nisi, ad iura quod attinet, obstet obex, ecclesiasticae communionis*

---

partenenza in voto alla Chiesa," in *Euntes Docete* 10 (1957), pp. 65-104; T. Zapelena, *De Ecclesia Christi,* II, 2nd ed. (Rome, 1954); C. García Extremeño, "La necesidad de la iglesia para salvarse," in *Studium* 3 (1963), pp. 31-86.

[24] I. Bonetti, "Il battesimo e l'appartenenza alla Chiesa," in *Stud. Patavina* 6 (1960), pp. 95-111; J. C. Groot, "Oecumenische reflexie op de kerk en haar zending in de wereld," in *Oecumene* 2 (1963), pp. 128-144; T. Jiménez Urresti, "Son Miembros de la Iglesia los Protestantes?" in *Rev. Esp. de Der. Canón.* 15 (1960), pp. 153-66; K. Mörsdorf, *Lehrbuch des Kirchenrechts,* 7th ed. (Paderborn, 1953); LThK VI, 2nd ed., cc. 222-3; U. Mosiek, "Die Zugehörigkeit zur Kirche im Rahmen der Kanonistik," in *Theol. und Glaube* 49 (1959), pp. 256-68; L. Richard, "Une thèse fondamentale de l'oecuménisme: le baptême, incorporation visible à l'Eglise," in *Nouv. Rev. Théol.* 74 (1952), pp. 485-92; E. Sauras, *op. cit.,* pp. 86-7; M. Schmaus, *Katholische Dogmatik,* III/1, 3rd ed. (Munich, 1958), p. 831. With special ref. to St. Thomas: C. E. O'Neill, "St. Thomas on the members of the Church," in *The Thomist* 27 (1963), esp. pp. 125-8; with emphasis on baptism as referring to the eucharist: H. Volk, "Das sakramenta Element in der Kirchengliedschaft," in *Unio Christianorum, Festschrift Archbp. L. Jäger* (Paderborn, 1962), pp. 345-57.

[25] Cf. in previous note: K. Mörsdorf, LThK VI, 2nd ed., and U. Mosiek.

vinculum impediens, vel lata ab Ecclesia censura). These canon-
ists identify *membrum* with *persona in Ecclesia.* The tendency of
this argument is better than the argument itself because the code
implies that, with baptism, the other conditions are also fulfilled.[26]

Theology, however, would find a more important argument in
a serious concentration on baptism as incorporation in Christ,
even for those baptized outside the Catholic Church. Their incorporation in Christ also entails in a certain measure incorporation in the Church of Christ. This widens the perspective of
the membership problem and also the question about salvation
"outside" the Church, because this brings out the whole issue
of the positive significance of non-Catholic Christian Churches.

VESTIGIA ECCLESIAE

In an allocution on the Eastern Churches of January 9, 1927,
Pius XI reminded his audience that "parts broken off a gold-
containing rock also contain gold".[27] Although this statement
did not explicitly refer to traditional theology, it nevertheless
brought to mind such theological expressions as *reliquiae* or
vestigia ecclesiae, which were already current in 16th century
controversies.[28] In Catholic theology the expression *vestigia ec-*

[26] Cf. K. Rahner, *Schriften zur Theologie,* II (Einsiedeln, 1955), pp.
23-6.

[27] *Osservatore Romano,* Jan. 10-11, 1927.

[28] Yves Congar, "A propos des 'vestigia Ecclesiae'," in *Vers l'unité
chrét.* 39 (1952), pp. 3-5; J. C. Dumont, "Vestigia Ecclesia," in *Vers
l'unité chrét.* 32 (1951), pp. 6-7; C. G. Extremeño, "La necesidad de la
iglesia para salvarse," in *Studium* 3 (1963), pp. 75-6; J. Hamer, "Le
baptême et l'Eglise; à propos des 'vestigia Ecclesiae'," in *Irénikon* 25
(1952), pp. 142-64 and 263-75; E. F. Hanahoe, "Vestigia Ecclesiae.
Their meaning and value," in *One Fold* (New York, 1959), pp. 272-83;
T. Sartory, *Die ökumenische Bewegung und die Einheit der Kirche*
(Meitingen, 1955), pp. 147-94; G. Thils, *Histoire doctrinale du mouvement oecuménique* (Louvain, 1955), pp. 142-7 and 183-97.

clesiae came again into use in order to describe elements of genuine ecclesial reality in non-Catholic Christian communities and Churches.

The occasion arose out of the Toronto Statement, a declaration by the central committee of the World Council of Churches at a congress held at Toronto, Ontario, July 1950.[29] This declaration invited Churches to recognize elements or *vestigia* of the true Church in other Churches in order to achieve a genuine dialogue with one another in the hope that these elements of truth would lead to the full truth and to a unity founded on the truth. Dumont, in his article (see footnote 28), was one of the first to adopt this line of thought in 1951. Particularly insofar as the Eastern Churches are concerned, the validity of their apostolic succession has never been queried, and consequently neither the validity of their episcopacy and their priesthood, nor the validity of their sacraments which goes with it. Where this apostolic succession has not usually been recognized, as in the Churches of the Reformation, there are other elements of the Christian heritage such as baptism and the preaching of the Word of God.

In 1955 Thils proved[30] that this was implicitly recognized even in the old apologetics when dealing with the Church. These older apologists, indeed, eliminated from the *nota ecclesiae* (the characteristic features of the true Church) everything the non-Catholic Christian communities and Churches had in common with the Catholic Church because such elements could not be used in the older form of apologetics. But this elimination implies recognition of authentic Christian values outside the Church of Rome and specifically in communities as such. This fact is expressed in the notion of "negative characteristic",[31] *i.e.,* a

[29] *Minutes and Reports of the Third Meeting of the Central Committee: Toronto, Canada* (Geneva, 1950).

[30] *Loc. cit.,* note 28.

[31] Cf. T. Zapelena, *De Ecclesia Christi. Pars apologetica,* 2nd ed. (Rome, 1950), p. 472.

characteristic that does not *exclusively* belong to the Church of Rome.

This possession of objective, genuine Christian realities makes it possible to assess in a more positive manner the "ecclesial" character of the Christian Churches not united with Rome.[32] It then follows that, because the faith of the individual non-Catholic Christian is determined by the faith and the sacramental reality of the communion to which he belongs and which contains positive elements of the Church of Christ, his redemption and sanctification do not take place *outside* his own communion, but precisely *by means of it*.

If the *votum ecclesiae* does not derive a clear and objective form from the *vestigia ecclesiae*, how can one interpret this *votum* otherwise than as a purely subjective value? Even the objective dynamic power of the *fides implicita*,[33] which contains, with the *votum baptismi*, also a *votum ecclesiae*, still demands a clearer expression of the bond with the Church.

THE "PAGAN" AND SALVATION

The most valuable efforts to achieve this clearer expression turn to the concept of the unity of mankind, so pronounced in

[32] Cf. S. Tromp, *De Spiritu Christi Anima* (Rome, 1960), pp. 196-7: "Quodsi consideramus Spiritum-Sanctum-Animam, ut *assimilantem* Corpori Mystico nova membra, vel quod ad idem redit, ut *proxime conducentem ad Christum:* adesse dicendus est in omnibus qui voto magis minusve explicito ad Ecclesiam ordinantur, sive agatur de personis *sive etiam de communitatibus*." The proposed schema *De Oecumenismo* for Vatican II is said to mention in Ch. 1 "ecclesiae et communitates separatae". The explanation added to it quotes many documents to show that "in traditione ecclesiastica nomen 'Ecclesiae' communitatibus orientalibus dissidentibus *saepe* et *constanter attribuitur*". Many Fathers of the Council have asked that the wording of the proposed text be changed into "ecclesiae et communitates ecclesiales a nobis separatae".

[33] P.-A. Liégé, "Le salut des 'autres'," in *Lum. et Vie* 18 (1954), pp. 741-69; Yves Congar, *La Sainte Eglise* (Paris, 1963), pp. 438-40.

patristic literature,[34] and the concomitant universal significance of the incarnation.[35] It is pointed out that within this one mankind, called to God, the laborious groping and seeking by "pagans" of goodwill represent the pilgrim situation of the Church. This seeking would be meaningless if there were no organic link with an already achieved plenitude. Precisely because this plenitude is already achieved in the Church, this seeking acquires an undeniable significance in the history of salvation as a whole: through the Church with which these "pagans" are invisibly linked, they undergo that vital influence that permeates the whole body.[36]

When one remembers the terminology used in connection with sacramental causality, one might say that the Church is a kind of "moral cause" of the salvation of "pagans". The same thought occurs when it is said that all grace always tends toward the Church.[37] This is usually argued as follows: God's will tends toward the Church. Since the "pagan" of goodwill wishes to do the will of God, he is also implicitly ordered toward the Church. Salvation is therefore granted these men for the Church's sake.[38]

A clear effort to penetrate into the "efficient causality" of the Church in the work of salvation begins by considering the implications of the human person's situation within the total unity of mankind. That an individual person is placed within the unity

[34] H. de Lubac, *Catholicisme,* 5th ed. (Paris, 1952); O. Semmelroth, *Die Kirche als Ursakrament* (Frankfurt, 1953).

[35] K. Rahner, "Die Gliedschaft in der Kirche nach der Lehre der Enzyklika Pius XII 'Mystici Corporis Christi'," in *Schriften zur Theologie* II (Einsiedeln, 1955), pp. 7-94. More or less on the same lines: J. Frisque, "Hors de l'Eglise il n'y a pas de salut," in *Eglise vivante* 7 (1955), pp. 98-107; A. Gommenginger, "Bedeutet die Exkommunikation Verlust der Kirchengliedschaft?" in *Zeitschr. f. Kath. Th.* 73 (1951), pp. 1-71; J. O'Connell, "The Salvation of non-Catholics," in *Downside Rev.* 72 (1954), pp. 256-63; cf. M. Eminyan, *The Theology of Salvation* (Boston, 1960).

[36] H. de Lubac, *loc. cit.* (note 34), ch. VII.

[37] O. Semmelroth, *loc. cit.* (note 34), p. 95.

[38] *Loc. cit.,* p. 142.

of mankind, is for that individual person a fact that precedes his free activity which he has to take into account.

As a person, every human being has to accept permanently this "natural" fact that he is bound up with the rest of mankind.[39] This human nature, which the person must express in his free activity, has received a special determination through the incarnation. Human nature is, in its very root, called to a supernatural participation in the life of God himself. This is a factual aspect of human nature, a definite, real and ontological dimension given to the nature of every human person.[40] Every free, concrete human action is therefore an acceptance or a denial of this directive, engraved in his being. In this way the concept becomes acceptable that there is a "People of God" co-extensive with mankind as a whole. This People of God underlies the juridical and social organization of what we call the Church, just as a given historical people underlies a given organized State.

MEMBERSHIP OF THE PEOPLE OF GOD

"Radically", "in his roots", therefore, every human being is already in the Church because membership of this People of God is already a factual aspect of human nature. Whenever a human being accepts the fact of his concrete human nature in his free actions, then his free action becomes at the same time the expression of God's saving will in grace. He thus accepts his membership in the People of God, which, in the unfolding of the incarnation, is the historical expression of God's saving will.

The action by which a man is redeemed can therefore rightly

[39] K. Rahner, loc. cit. (note 35), pp. 85-7. Cf. K. Riesenhuber, "Der anonyme Christ, nach Karl Rahner," in Zeitschr. f. Kath. Th. 86 (1964), pp. 286-303.
[40] Loc. cit., p. 88.

be called a *votum ecclesiae*, first, because it implicitly tends toward the Church, just as in all people there is a tendency toward the formation of a State; and secondly, because it implies a positive acceptance of that part of the Church that coincides with membership in the People of God. Because of this second reason the free action by which man positively accepts the implications of his concrete nature, may even be said to be of a quasi-sacramental kind.[41]

Although this view does not explain everything either, it is the most powerful effort to rise above terminological distinctions and to reach theological intelligibility. It still is not clear what the relation is between what is here called the People of God and the one sacramental Church which is meant in the expression *extra ecclesiam nulla salus*.[42] Nor is it clear yet whether the reality which, in concrete human nature, results from the call to participation in God's life, is a supernatural and "ecclesial" reality.[43] In this connection a distinction is made between the *votum ecclesiae* and the *votum salvificum* (the saving desire).[44] The latter is only present when, in his general attitude, the person assents to the objective *votum ecclesiae*.

The two, indeed, need not coincide as is clear, for instance, in the case of what is called "formal heresy". Thus, the objective *votum ecclesiae* does not always include the *votum salvificum*, but the *votum salvificum* always includes the *votum ecclesiae*. The *votum salvificum*, which implies the *votum ecclesiae*, lies, for the "pagan" who has received God's grace, in his supernatural faith and his acting charity,[45] both of which, according to constant tradition, can also be granted by God outside the

[41] *Loc. cit.*, pp. 89-91.

[42] B. A. Willems, "De algemene heilsoorzakelijkheid van de kerk," in *Jaarboek kath. theol. in Ned.* (1962), pp. 38-40.

[43] C. G. Extremeño, "La necesidad de la iglesia para salvarse," in *Studium* 3 (1963), pp. 83-4.

[44] *Id., ibid.*, pp. 67-86.

[45] *Loc. cit.*, p. 77.

framework of the sacraments. In this active faith there lies an objective orientation toward the Church, whether one is explicitly conscious of it or not. The expression *extra ecclesiam nulla salus,* then, does not mean to concentrate on the boundaries of the Church but rather on the universal mediatory role of Christ's Church.[46]

VOCATION TO VICARIOUSNESS

The way in which the Church exercises her universal mediation has been elucidated by the biblical notion of "vicariousness".[47] Insofar as the subjective conditions for salvation are concerned, Scripture mentions two complementary points. In the first place, he who has love has everything (Matt. 22, 35-40; Rom. 13, 9ff.; Matt. 25, 31-46). The attitude toward one's fellowman is decisive for salvation or damnation.[48] On the other hand, the Scriptures teach that no one really has this love because every man lies imprisoned in his own selfishness. Every man, therefore, should be damned (Rom. 3, 23). This, however, does not happen because of the vicarious character of Christ's superabundant love. The real decision lies thus with love, but because man's love is always deficient, he must also "believe", which means that he must stand open for Christ.

This faith, required for salvation, is therefore the opposite of human self-sufficiency; it is the loving admission of one's own

[46] *Loc. cit.,* p. 70. See also L. Scipioni, "La Chiesa causa necessaria e universale della salvezza," in *Sacra Doctr.* 5 (1960), pp. 256-89.

[47] J. Ratzinger, "Die neuen Heiden und die Kirche," in *Hochland* 51 (1958), pp. 1-11; *id.,* "Stellvertretung," in *Handb. theol. Grundbegr.* II (Munich, 1963), pp. 566-75; *id.,* "Salus extra Ecclesiam nulla est," in *DO-C,* Oct. 28, 1963; L. Scheffczyk, "Die heilshafte stellvertretung als missionarischer Impuls," in *Geist und Leben* 37 (1964), pp. 104-25.

[48] See also Yves Congar, *Ausser der Kirche kein Heil* (Essen, 1961); B. A. Willems, "De kerk en haar plaats in het heilsbestel," in *Tijds. v. Theol.* 3 (1963), pp. 75-83.

impotence and a willingness to receive the help of that Other. This willingness may be called *votum ecclesiae,* yet this is but part of a whole which receives its full meaning only from the objective fact of the vicariousness of the *Christus totus.*[49] In fact, the whole of mankind lives only through the vicarious service of Jesus Christ. It is the Church's vocation to participate in this vicariousness. The Church is not an exclusive group of those that are saved, but the communion of those that are called to live in service of the many. Therefore, one can in a similar manner speak of the Church as a vanguard in which that anonymous Christianity which exists also outside the Church has found itself, has become socially accessible and has thus become the *signum elevatum in nationibus* (the sign raised among the nations).[50]

The widening of the problem from the individual to the communal which becomes evident here has also been logically applied to a re-appreciation of pagan religions.[51] Some scholars even wonder whether the traditional habit of speaking of "ordinary" and "extraordinary" ways of salvation should not be reversed. The Church is the extraordinary way because the majority of mankind does not come to salvation inside the Church. Nevertheless, the call to all to translate their anonymous Christianity in terms of the special revelation of the Church remains in force. This, in the first place, because, in the concrete, grace

[49] J. Ratzinger, "Stellvertretung," *loc. cit.* (note 47), pp. 574-5.

[50] K. Rahner, "Dogmatische Randbemerkungen zur 'Kirchenfrömmigkeit'," in *Sentire Ecclesiam* (Freiburg, 1961), pp. 9-44 (= *Schriften zur Theologie* V, pp. 379-410).

[51] K. Rahner, "Das Christentum und die nichtchristlichen Religionen," in *Pluralismus, Toleranz und Christenheit* (Nuremberg, 1961), pp. 55-74 (= *Schriften zur Theologie* V, pp. 136-158); H. R. Schlette, *Die Religionen als Thema der Theologie* (Freiburg, 1964); *id.,* "Thesen zum Selbstverst andnis der Theologie angesichts der Religionen," in *Gott in Welt* II (Freiburg, 1964) pp. 306-16; *id.,* "Religionen," in *Handb. theol. Grundbegr.* II (Munich, 1963), pp. 441-450; M. Vereno, "Von der All-Wirklichkeit der Kirche," in *Theol. Quartalschrift* 138 (1958), pp. 385-427.

and Christianity involve incarnation, and secondly, because a clearer and more conscious understanding of what may already be present anonymously, offers greater opportunities for the individual person. Communion and consequently salvation are better fulfilled when what is communally present has received a name and become explicit.

THE CALL TO GRACE

It is clear that in this question the place and significance of *fides implicita* are of paramount importance. St. Thomas held that since the incarnation an explicit faith in the principal truths of revelation was necessary for salvation. His view seems rather strict but some explain this by pointing out that his knowledge of the geographical spreading of the Gospel was somewhat defective.[52] Others, however, point out that according to St. Thomas every man in actual fact sins or is saved through the grace of God when he first acts as an adult human being.[53]

Continuing along the same lines some scholars argue that the first moral action of every man includes implicit faith or the opposite.[54] God's anticipating grace operates always and not merely occasionally in order to draw all men toward their supernatural goal.[55] This enduring call to grace by God is not some-

[52] J. Taschner, *Die Notwendigkeit des ausdrücklichen Glaubens an Christus* (Kaldenkirchen, 1960).

[53] *Summa Theol.*, Ia IIae, q. 89, a. 6.

[54] J. Maritain, *Neuf leçons sur les notions premières de la philosophie morale* (Téqui, 1951); *id.*, "La dialectique immanente du premier acte de liberté," in *Nova et Vetera* 20 (1945), pp. 218-35. Cf. D. Grasso, "La nécessité de la foi au Christ pour le salut. Foi implicite et acte de contrition," in *Christ au Monde* 5 (1959), pp. 75-82; Dict. *Catholicisme* IV, 1388. A. Santos Hernandez's criticism (*op. cit.*, pp. 599-600), based on the experience of the non-believer, does not seem to take enough account of the *implicit* character of this offer of grace.

[55] G. de Broglie, "Possibilité et impossibilité de la 'foi naturelle'," in *Rech. de Sc. Rel.* 52 (1964), pp. 5-41.

thing extrinsic to man. It has therefore been suggested that man's *instinctus naturae* becomes itself the *instinctus fidei* in man's concrete situation by virtue of God's continuous creative act.[56] In this way the question of the salvation of those who never had the Gospel preached to them receives a rather radical solution.

The question remains, though, whether this argument does full justice, not to the *separation* of the natural order and the order of grace (because these are not separated in the concrete), but to the *distinction* between these two orders.[57] The point where man's supernatural vocation connects with human nature is precisely grace itself. It does not remain extrinsic to man because man's nature stands open to the supernatural. This does not mean, therefore, that in actual fact man has ever lived in a purely natural condition, but that the recognition of man's concrete existence as an offer of God's grace is not rooted in himself, but in God's free saving will that is directed to all men without exception.

Some scholars have developed this last point and have reached a far-reaching re-appreciation of the traditional opinion about the salvation of children who have died without baptism.[58]

[56] M. Seckler, "Das Heil der Nichtevangelisierten in thomistischer Sicht," in *Tüb. theol. Quartalschr.* 140 (1960), pp. 39-69; *id., Instinkt und Glaubenswille* (Mainz, 1961); O. Pesch, "Instinkt und Glaubenswille," in *Catholica* 16 (1962), pp. 69-77.

[57] Cf. J. Alfaro, "Supernaturalitas fidei," in *Greg.* 44 (1963), pp. 501-42; *id.,* "Transcendencia e immanencia de lo sobrenatural," in *Greg.* 38 (1957), pp. 5-50; E. Schillebeeckx, "Het niet-begrippelijk moment in de geloofsdaad volgens Thomas van Aquino," in *Tijdschr. v. Theol.* 3 (1963), pp. 167-95.

[58] The literature on this problem is so plentiful that it would require a bibliographical survey by itself. We limit ourselves to the following: A. Beni, "Si salvano i Bambini morti senza battesimo?" in *Città di Vita* (1960), pp. 10-20; *id., La vera Chiesa* (Florence, 1953); M. Diekhaus, "A sorte eterna das crianças não-batizadas," in *Rev. Eccl. Brasil.* 16 (1956), pp. 17-25; G. J. Dyer, "A Theological Evaluation," in *Theol. Stud.* 19 (1958), pp. 32-49; *id., Limbo: unsettled question* (New York, 1964); P. Gumpel, "Unbaptized Infants, may they be saved?" in *Downside Rev.* 72 (1954), pp. 342-458; *id.,* "Unbaptized Infants. A further Report," in *Downside Rev.* 73 (1955), pp. 317-46; A. Hastings, "The

Salvation of unbaptized infants," in *Downside Rev.* 77 (1959), pp. 172-8; Ch.-V. Héris, "Enfants (salut des)," in Dict. *Catholicisme* IV, cc. 151-7; L. Kruse, "Die Stellungnahme des Konzils von Trient zur Angesicht Cajetans über die Kinderersatztaufe in konzilsgeschichtlicher und theologiegeschichtlicher Gegenwartsbedeutung," in *Catholica* 14 (1960), pp. 55-77; M. Laurenge, "Esquisses d'une étude sur le sort des enfants morts sans baptême," in *L'Année théol. august.* 12 (1952), pp. 145-85; H. de Lavalette, "Autour de la question des enfants morts sans baptême," in *Nouv. Rev. théol.* 92 (1960), pp. 56-69; A. Pacios López, "La suerte de los niños muertos sin bautismo," in *Rev. Esp. de Teol.* 14 (1954), pp. 41-58; A. Perego, "Esiste un sostituvo del battesimo per la giustificazione dei bambini?" in *Divinitas* 4 (1960), pp. 561-74; A. Santos Hernandez, *Salvación y Paganismo* (Santander, 1960), pp. 621-710; L. Renwart, "Le baptême des enfants et les limbes," in *Nouv. Rev. théol.* 80 (1958), pp. 449-67; B. Webb, "Unbaptized Infants and the Quasi-Sacrament of Death," in *Downside Rev.* 71 (1953), pp. 243-7.

PART III

DO-C DOCUMENTATION
CONCILIUM

On November 15, 1963 a meeting was held in Rome between the "International DO-C", section of the "DO-C, Dutch Documentation Center for the Council", and the Board of Editors of CONCILIUM. The following agreement was reached:

The "International DO-C", known for the important work of theological information during the Council periods, is prepared to place itself completely at the disposition of CONCILIUM and to furnish every volume with theological information in keeping with the most urgent needs of the Church. For this purpose Part III of each volume of CONCILIUM has been set up under the name of "DO-C: Documentation Concilium".

In this section the editors of CONCILIUM will follow step-by-step the daily development of theological thinking, giving a survey of the historical background, the various opinions, trends and experiences that are at the heart of the living Church.

In this first volume of CONCILIUM, Documentation Concilium presents the historical background of Eucharistic Congresses and also treats of the dialogue between the Church and contemporary cultures.

Leo Alting von Geusau, *Director*
M. J. Le Guillou, O. P., *Asst. Director*

ROGER AUBERT

Born in Ixelles-Bruxelles in 1914, he is today **a** doctor of philosophy and theology. After teaching in the seminary at Malines, Belgium, from 1944 to 1952, he came to his present post at the university of Louvain, Belgium, where he teaches church history. In 1945 he published his doctoral thesis, "Le problème de l'acte de foi". His numerous activities and many published works concentrate upon the problems of contemporary church history. Examples are: *Le Saint Siège et l'union des Eglises; Le Pontificat de Pie IX* (Vol. XXI in Fliche-Martin); *La théologie catholique au milieu du XX*ᵉ *siècle* (1953); *Problèmes de l'unité chrétienne* (1955); *Le concile du Vatican* (Vol. XII in *l'Histoire des conciles oecuméniques sous la direction de G. Dumeige, 1964*).

Roger Aubert/*Louvain, Belgium*

Eucharistic Congresses from Leo XIII to Paul VI

From the middle of the 19th century there was evidence throughout Europe, particularly in France, of an astonishing number of movements directed to promoting the worship of the Blessed Sacrament. This renewal of eucharistic piety, a reaction against Jansenist severity and the attacks of atheism, took different forms, but more often than not the emphasis fell on the cult of adoration and even more frequently on reparation to Jesus Christ, the God hidden beneath the appearances of the host, outraged by impiety, ignored by governments which aimed at the secularization of society. It was in this latter perspective that, about 1875, the idea of the international Eucharistic Congress was born.[1]

[1] On the first Eucharistic Congresses, see J. Vaudon, *L'Oeuvre des Congrès Eucharistiques, ses origines* (Paris, 1910); L. de Paladini, *Die Eucharistische Kongresse, Ursprung und Geschichte* (Paderborn, 1912). For the beginnings, see in particular M. de Hedouville, *Mgr. de Ségur* (Paris, 1957), ch. XIX. For later development, see E. Lesne, "Du Congrès Eucharistique International de Lille en 1881 au Congrès National de Lille en 1931," in *Cinquantenaire des Congrès Eucharistiques Internationaux* (Lille, 1931).

At the origin of these Congresses is to be found the initiative and perseverance of a holy woman, Mlle. Tamisier, who was encouraged by one of the chief apostles of eucharistic devotion in the France of that day, Msgr. Gaston de Ségur. They dreamed of adding to the silent adoration of the Blessed Sacrament, which had become so widespread in the previous quarter-century, magnificent spectacles that would bring to the indifferent masses a realization of the eucharistic presence at the same time as they gave to Catholics, made timid by persecution, the sense of their own numbers and strength.

The first idea was to make use of the revived interest in pilgrimages by organizing pilgrimages of reparation to the principal sanctuaries where a eucharistic miracle had occurred. Several local attempts were made from 1874 to 1877; with the help of sermons and the pamphlets that Mlle. Tamisier distributed, these efforts gradually familiarized the Catholic people with a new type of large-scale demonstration. However, she quickly conceived the idea of adding to them study sessions that would turn them into real Congresses, and to accomplish their end these Congresses were to have not merely a national but an international audience.

EARLY LACK OF SUPPORT

These still rather vague plans were communicated to Leo XIII in April, 1879 and the Pope blessed the enterprise. But nearly everything remained to be done in the way of concrete realization, and circumstances could hardly have been more unfavorable. Since 1877 radicals had seized the direction of the government in France with the words of Gambetta as their motto: "Clericalism is the enemy!" With the prospect of rising storms, bishops thought it imprudent to arouse the adversaries of the

Church by becoming patrons of noisy demonstrations destined to recall the rights of Christ in public life.

Nor was Mlle. Tamisier able to find any support among the religious orders: the Assumptionist Fathers, specialists in large-scale pilgrimages since 1870, did not wish to add anything further to their many undertakings; the Fathers of the Blessed Sacrament were "more suited to prayer than external activity"; the Jesuits of Paray-le-Monial, though favorably inclined in principle, nevertheless did not dare show open support because of the threats being formulated against their own Society.

It was then that Mlle. Tamisier thought of turning to Catholic Belgium, where eucharistic devotion was so intense, and in September of 1880 she contacted Cardinal Deschamps. But here, too, political circumstances—Belgium was in the midst of the school controversy—seemed to make postponement advisable. An approach to the Netherlands was even less successful: the bishops were far from enthusiastic about the idea of seeing French Catholics, much too excitable to their way of thinking, hold a meeting in Holland; moreover, they distrusted this initiative on the part of the laity which was receiving such lukewarm support from the hierarchy.

Msgr. de Ségur, convinced that they would have no success unless the initial impulse came from Rome, obtained Cardinal Deschamps' promise to intervene once more with Leo XIII, and the Pope repeated the expression of the keen interest he felt in the project, without, however, deciding (in spite of urging from several other persons) on any concrete action destined to bring about the realization of the plan in the immediate future. No doubt he feared that anticlerical governments, with which relations were already strained, would consider as a provocation any direct encouragement to organize an international Catholic Congress.

A new disappointment was soon added to the previous ones:

Msgr. de Ségur's health rapidly deteriorated, and in March of 1881 he was obliged to give up any further active support of the enterprise. All seemed lost, at least for the moment, when an unforeseen event occurred. A sympathizer close to the movement suggested that an appeal be made to the Catholics of the north of France, where eucharistic piety was flourishing under the impulse of the great industrialist of Lille, Philibert Vrau, and where for some years regional Catholic Congresses had been organized. By return post Monsieur Vrau let it be understood that he and his associates would undertake the project. Something more modest than what Mlle. Tamisier had in mind would be attempted, but at least it would be a beginning.

THE TIDE TURNS: FIRST CONGRESS

Good progress was made from this moment on. The organizers had decided to suppress any exterior demonstration and it was easy for them to obtain the authorization of the Archbishop of Cambrai.[2] On April 25 a circular was issued inviting the Catholics of the whole world to a Eucharistic Congress to be held at Lille at the end of June. The following month, Monsieur Vrau, accompanied by the Vicomte de Damas, went to Rome and with the invaluable help of Père Picard of the Assumptionist Fathers obtained official approbation from Leo XIII.

Preparation for this first Congress had to be completed in two months' time, but participation in it, however modest (363 persons, 200 from the area and 100 from Paris), surpassed expectations and had a symbolically international character since in addition to 36 Belgians there were 11 foreign delegates representing 8 different countries. The final procession inside the Church of Notre Dame de la Treille was a success because of the spontaneous addition to the Congress members of 4000 men from the city.

[2] At this period Lille had not been erected into a diocese.

For three days the members had listened to many reports in three different sections: adoration and reparation; worship and exterior acts of homage; propaganda (that is, a review of eucharistic works in existence in France and abroad). In the evening they met in plenary session where the royalist deputy from Belcastel and Père Lemann, a convert from Judaism, proclaimed the rights of Christ in public life. This was only a trial run, but the framework of future Congresses was henceforth established, and, satisfied with the results, the promoters decided to give a periodic character to the movement and immediately set up a permanent committee.

Msgr. de Ségur, who would have been the logical choice for Chairman of this committee, had died three weeks before. The choice fell on Bishop de la Bouillerie, coadjutor Bishop of Bordeaux, for thirty years an active organizer of eucharistic devotions; two vice-chairmen from Paris who had served as intermediaries with the Catholics of Lille were added: Monsieur de Benque, who had been at Mlle. Tamisier's side from the beginning, and Comte de Nicolay. From the sociological point of view, they emphasized the atmosphere of "old France" in which the movement had found its initial supporters.

PROCESSIONS BEGIN: CIVIC PARTICIPATION

In the following year a second Congress took place at Avignon, where Mlle. Tamisier had organized small eucharistic pilgrimages in 1874 and 1876 and where the Confraternity of Gray Penitents, who were very active, could furnish support similar to that of the Catholics in the north. The impetus had now been given, and since Rome no longer hid its encouragement, Bishop Doutreloux of Liège, who, in spite of his own desires had not dared to yield to the request of Mlle. Tamisier in 1881, declared his readiness to receive the members of the Congress in 1883. In this region,

which was very proud of its public liberties, where public manifestations, even religious ones, were safe from the ban of munici-
pal authorities, it was at last possible to organize the solemn
procession envisaged by the promoters in the beginning as the
best means of carrying into the social sphere the cult of the
Blessed Sacrament and giving spectacular affirmation to the
Catholic faith in the mystery of the Real Presence, the target of
the jeers of the positivist intelligentsia of the period.

To give greater emphasis to the international character of the
Congress, Bishop Mermillod of Fribourg (Switzerland) was
named President; he had been sympathetic to the movement from
the very beginning and organized the 4th Congress in his episcopal see in 1885. On this occasion and in this officially Catholic
canton, the civil authorities, the government, the judiciary, even
the army—salutes from the cannon accented the public prayers
—took an active part in the ceremonies of the Congress, in which
the theme of the social overlordship of Christ was exhaustively
studied. It was a splendid triumph and hearts rejoiced to see
again "as in the ages of faith", Jesus Christ honored as temporal
king.

After Fribourg, the Congress returned to France: at Toulouse
in 1886, in Paris (at last) in 1888, then once more in Belgium
at Antwerp in 1890, where for the first time a language other
than French was used in some of the reports. But the new President, Bishop Doutreloux, had won the approval of the members
—now more than 1400 in number—for the promise to associate
the Eastern Churches with their activities in the future. Accordingly, in 1893 the 8th Congress was held in Jerusalem at the
invitation of Leo XIII himself, who, in this celebration at the
very site of the Last Supper, saw an opportunity to show the
eucharist, which the Eastern schismatics had kept at the center
of their worship, as the sacrament of reconciliation that restores,
amid a diversity of rites, the great unity of the Catholic world.

The Congress at Jerusalem

This is not the place to show the unparalleled importance of this Congress at Jerusalem in the endeavors for union carried on by Leo XIII and in the re-discovery by Catholics of the venerable specificity of the Eastern rites.[3] From the point of view proper to the Eucharistic Congresses, it is an important date for two reasons: first, because of the broadening of geographical horizons, although this Congress was long to remain without a sequel and we must not forget how thoroughly at home Frenchmen felt at that time in the Levant; and secondly, on the plane of structural organization, by reason of the more direct intervention of the Holy See.

In fact, not only was it Leo XIII who directed the members of the Congress to Jerusalem, but, in order to emphasize the exceptional significance he attached to the move, he appointed as papal legate, Cardinal Langenieux, Archbishop of Rheims. The Pope was to repeat this gesture twice more in 1898 and 1902 at the 12th and 14th Congresses, and soon, under St. Pius X, the custom of having each Congress presided over by a papal legate was established.

The accession of Pius X, the "Pope of the Eucharist", coincided with the nomination of a new and particularly enterprising president, Bishop Heylen, the polyglot Bishop of Namur. This date opens a new stage in the history of the Congresses, principally in their exterior development. With its 5000 members the Congress of Namur (1902) already gave evidence of an increase which henceforth was to continue. At Lourdes, in 1914, there were 10 cardinals and 200 bishops, as many as the sum total of Congress members from outside the diocese of Cambrai at the first meeting. This very success modified to some extent the origi-

---

[3] On the importance of the Jerusalem Congress from the point of view of reunion, see R. Esposito, *Leone XIII et l'Oriente cristiano* (Rome, 1960), pp. 367-84.

nal character, to the regret of more than one person, for exterior manifestations of faith and enthusiasm were progressively, and fatally, to claim attention to the detriment of the study sessions. On the other hand, the truly international character was to receive palpable increase.

BROADENING HORIZONS

Of the first 15 Congresses, 9 were held in France, 4 in Belgium, and 1 in Switzerland, countries considered in some sense a prolongation of France, and even in Jerusalem the presence of the French was very marked. Beginning in 1905, the 25th anniversary of the foundation of the movement, Pius X decided that the Congress would be held in Rome, and would be presided over by the Sovereign Pontiff himself. He would celebrate the opening pontifical mass and would preach at the closing ceremonies. Then, after the interim Congress at Tournai in 1906, he named as successive sites for the Congresses three cities in predominantly Protestant countries: Metz, then under German rule, in 1907; London, in 1908; Cologne, in 1909.

In the following year, if the Congress could be held in a Catholic country where political and social authorities would participate actively (as they had in Fribourg), it was to be overseas in Montreal. Then, with the Congress at Madrid in 1911 and in Vienna in 1912, two more new countries would be added to the list, and the importance of foreign delegations would be correspondingly increased. This broadening of the horizon was all the more imperative in that, as a direct outcome of systematic propaganda, national Eucharistic Congresses had been organized practically everywhere. It was important, from this time on, that international Congresses should be distinguished from national ones by a resolutely worldwide character.

Some points of their orientation were also to be changed. It is certain that the early concerns could not disappear; on the contrary, the Congresses would remain what they had been intended to be from the beginning, namely, public manifestations destined to stimulate the faith of Catholics in the Real Presence and their zeal for all forms of adoration of the Blessed Sacrament, to shatter their human respect, and to proclaim aloud the kingship of Christ which is rejected by the devotees of secularism.

GROWTH FROM WITHIN: FREQUENT COMMUNION

From this point of view the ceremonies in Madrid and above all in Vienna, where the Emperor and the Archdukes followed the procession in dress uniform in the midst of a throng numbering hundreds of thousands of persons, constituted a climax that made a deep impression. But it was possible to see moving into the foreground, with ever greater clarity, another aspect that had scarcely appeared in the time of Leo XIII: the concern to encourage frequent and even daily reception of holy communion. Pius X made systematic use of the Congresses to prepare the reception, and then to favor the diffusion and implementation of his famous eucharistic decrees.

Under the spell of orators like the Belgian Jesuit Lintelo, publicly encouraged by the papal legates, the Congresses were instrumental in the formation in different countries of men's leagues for regular reception of the sacrament and of the "Eucharistic Crusade" for children. Springing from the pious initiative of the laity, these became a powerfully effective means of action for the Holy See, to remind men that the eucharist, while it is an object of worship, is essentially a food.

World War I interrupted the movement. Benedict XV desired to see its resumption at the earliest feasible date so that, if possible, in a country that had remained neutral, all Catholics might give one another the "kiss of peace in the presence of Jesus in the sacrament of the altar". But organization got under way very slowly, and it was finally at Rome in 1922, at the beginning of the pontificate of Pius XI, that the tradition was continued, giving primacy to a new idea: the sacrament as symbol of union among men and the sole means of realizing it on this earth.

In accord with the decision of Rome, Congresses were to be held henceforth every two years, the assertion of claims against the secular state yielding more and more to a positive witness of faith in the Christian mystery: at Amsterdam, in 1924, where certain Protestants noisily insisted on the contrast between the modest entry of Christ into Jerusalem and the luxurious limousines of the papal legate and the cardinals; at Chicago, in 1926, where were gathered one-fourth of the sacred college and 550 bishops; at Sydney in Australia, in 1928, where the Congress was closed by an impressive blessing of the ocean; at Carthage, in 1930, in the heart of Moslem territory, where enthusiasts believed they saw a presage of the spiritual rebirth of the Africa of St. Augustine; at Dublin, in 1932, witness to the explosive fervor of an entire nation; at Buenos Aires, in 1934, the first attempt in Latin America; at Manila in 1936; at Budapest in 1938. Once more, war interrupted the series, and it was necessary to wait until 1952 before the next Congress opened at Barcelona; followed, at four-year intervals, by the Congresses of Rio de Janeiro (1956) and Munich (1960).

The Liturgical Movement: Ecumenical Development

Something new, symptomatic of a change of minds, appeared in the first postwar Congress: whereas up to this point the final procession constituted the climax of what had seemed like "a worldwide Corpus Christi celebration" and low masses had allowed participants to satisfy their religious obligations, henceforth the mass took its place at the center of all the demonstrations. The liturgical movement was beginning to bear fruit.

For the rest, in spite of certain interesting initiatives—for example, the organization of a day consecrated to bringing to the most abandoned invalids some sign of fraternal affection—the Barcelona Congress remained in the tradition of the period between the two wars: it was the manifestation of the piety of the nation in which it was held, closed by the consecration of Spain to the Blessed Sacrament by General Franco, and delegations from foreign countries, however numerous, seemed scarcely more than honored guests.

Even at Munich, where the national element was less conspicuous, it was regrettable that the Congress remained more a juxtaposition of national pilgrimages rather than a real international Catholic encounter that would facilitate the experience of international solidarity among Christians. On the other hand, from certain points of view the Munich Congress marked an interesting development. First of all, care was taken to have the Congress operate in an ecumenical atmosphere, seeking to avoid wounding Protestant sensibilities and to put the emphasis on points shared in common. This was a program that would have seemed paradoxical in earlier Congresses, at the opposite pole from a "Reformation" climate, but which was made possible by two things: the clear directive from Cardinal Doepfner to avoid all displays of power in spite of the presence of a million participants in the closing ceremonies, and to concentrate rather on the humble attempt to plumb the depths of the mysteries of faith; and even more by the effort to integrate in the highest possible degree in the contemporary liturgical renewal a manifestation of piety that had its roots in forms of devotion typical of the 19th century, and thus to reconcile two movements that had long been opposed to one another.

LIVING THE PASCHAL MYSTERY

Not only was every effort made to emphasize in reports and commentaries how every form of eucharistic piety has its real meaning only with reference to the sacrifice of Christ, but ceremonies were organized so as to have the participants live from day to day through the various phases of the paschal mystery, the heart of the liturgical year, and, in particular, the central position of the mass, celebrated in admirable communal fashion, was emphasized.

Moreover, Father Jungmann wished to provide a new vision of Eucharistic Congresses to those who found their original theological raison d'être outmoded, and to have them appear henceforth as a sort of semi-official liturgical celebration of the Church. He therefore suggested looking upon these demonstrations, culminating in the celebration of the mass by the papal legate and moving from one city to another over the whole face of the earth, as a resumption on the scale of the universal Church of the ancient practice in which the bishop, especially at Rome, in order to express the unity of his diocese over and above its division into parishes, used to celebrate the eucharistic sacrifice in each of the churches in turn.

The *Statio Orbis* would thus replace the ancient *Statio Urbis*. This original idea did not fail to command attention particularly from the Orthodox.[4] In any case, it has the advantage of emphasizing the fact that Eucharistic Congresses must have as their essential object the reunion of the faithful of the entire world for the common celebration of the eucharistic banquet.

[4] See J. Jungmann, "Corpus Mysticum: Gedanken zum kommenden Eucharistischen Weltkongress," in *Stimmen der Zeit* CLXIV (1958-9), pp. 401-9, and the comments of N. Afanassieff, "Statio Orbis," in *Irénikon* XXXV (1962), pp. 65-75. Readers will be interested in the penetrating reflections of J. Ratzinger, "Der Eucharistische Weltkongress im Spiegel der Kritik," in *Statio Orbis: Eucharistischer Weltkongress 1960 in München* I (Munich, 1961), pp. 227-42.

How will this institution of the Eucharistic Congress continue to evolve and accomplish its own *aggiornamento?* It is not the historian's task to reply to this question, but we can rest assured that the living Church will be able to find an adequate response.

RAPHAEL VAN KETS, O.P.

Born in Drongen, Belgium in 1924, he became a Dominican in Ghent, and was ordained in 1950. He taught philosophy at the regional seminary in Niangara, Congo, and then continued his philosophical studies at the Angelicum in Rome. He earned his doctorate with the thesis, "De functie van de katholieke godsdienst in de vorming van de Kongolese gemeenschap" (the function of the Catholic religion in the forming of the community of the Congo), which was published in 1963 under the title "De Kongolese mens en zijn toekomst" (the man of the Congo and his future). In 1964 he was appointed professor of ethics and cultural anthropology at the Angelicum in Rome.

Raphael Van Kets, O. P. / *Rome, Italy*

The Dialogue
between the Church
and Contemporary Cultures

One of the great problems of our time is the relationship between the Church and the contemporary world. A schema about this subject—the original schema XVII—has been prepared for the Council. In the encyclical *Ecclesiam Suam* this subject receives more extensive treatment than any other. Significantly it underlines the necessity of the "dialogue" for the relationship between the Church and the world. This dialogue takes place in relationships that are determined by numerous and often very complex elements, and the deceptively simple statement that "Church and world must maintain a dialogue with each other" contains in fact one of the most demanding tasks for both the religious sense and the thinking mind of man.

In this consideration of the relation between Church and world, the relations between Church and culture on the one hand, and those between the Church and contemporary cultures on the other, play an important part. The problem of the relation between Church and culture deals with its basic relation to culture as such; its relation to contemporary cultures deals more

specifically with the diversity of these cultures and its consequences. Theoretically these problems can be separated, but in
practice they are but one. Every culture, indeed, springs from
the same basic factor: man's search for a full, truly human existence. Cultural diversity is but a consequence of the historical
development of various cultural groups. "La personne humaine
établit une unité entre les diverses civilisations; c'est l'homme qui
enjambe successivement, à travers les siècles, les tombeaux des
civilisations mortes et donne à leur histoire une unité que l'histoire
ne comporte pas." [1]

The inquiry into the essence and structure of culture is far
from completed. The understanding of human culture cannot
run ahead of the scientific study of man, and on many points this
scientific study is still very young. [2]

The distinction between religion and culture is relatively recent, at least in the cultural groups of the West. In other groups,
such as the Islamic ones, religion and culture coincide. [3] The
increasingly emphasized distinction, however, between the religious community and the natural one, which one can observe in
the West and which many consider a definite gain to civilization,
is also growing in those cultures where the religious and cultural
elements are still closely intertwined. It is thought that this is
mainly due to the influence of a technological society. [4]

The history of the Catholic Church clearly shows a constant
tension between this world and the other, between flight from
the world and openness to the world. According to various periods

[1] R. P. Delos, O.P., "Valeur des Civilisations et Apport Chrétien," in
Peuples d'Outre-Mer et Civilisation Occidentale (Semaines Sociales de
France, XXXV, 1948).
[2] For a survey, see Krech, Crutchfiel, Ballachey, Individual in Society
(New York-London, 1962).
[3] L'Eglise et les Civilisations (Semaine des Intellectuels Catholiques
Français, ed. P. Horay, Paris, 1955). "Approche des non-Chrétiens," in
Informations Catholiques Internationales (August, 1964), pp. 221-222.
This contains the main bibliography in French for the most recent years.
[4] Les Grandes Religions face au Monde d'Aujourd'hui (Recherche et
Débats, Cahier 37, Dec. 1961).

of its history there have been tendencies that inclined to either one or other extreme. Today, more than ever before, we look for a balance. The papal encyclical points the way: to be in the world but not of the world. "When there is a distinction between the Church and mankind, it is not in order to oppose them but in order to unite them." [5] The problems created by the tension that links the Church to contemporary cultures are easily perceived on perusal of the papal encyclical.

It is not our intention to give here a commentary on *Ecclesiam Suam*. Such a commentary must be preceded by some understanding of the relationship between the Church and contemporary cultures.

First of all, there is the concept of culture. It is not necessary to repeat the rejection of the opinion that culture is a mere biological phenomenon. As Herskovits puts it plainly: "La culture est ce qui dans le milieu est dû à l'homme." [6] Some still distinguish between culture and civilization. In this case, culture would be "la forme communautaire historique d'un peuple comme d'un tout" (Utz) and civilization the activity "qui concourt à structurer et à organiser une société de façon à ce qu'un hiérarchie de valeurs y soit respectée et admise" (Birou). According to this opinion culture is rather a sociological reality while civilization is what culture aims at. This (abstract) distinction, like that between culture as the spiritual, and civilization as the material and technical, development of a people, is increasingly abandoned today. [7]

Sociological forms and values, spiritual and material-technical data are difficult to separate in spite of the fact that, for instance, technical progress is not always accompanied by many-sided achievements of the mind, or *vice versa*. Within each culture the

---

[5] Free translation by the translator, in the absence of an official English version.

[6] M. J. Herskovits, *Les bases de l'Anthropologie Culturelle* (Payot, Paris, 1952), p. 6. Cf. Kaj. Birket-Smith, *Geschichte der Kultur* (Zurich, 1948).

[7] Cf. A. Cuvilier, *Manuel de Sociologie*, II (P.U.F., Paris, 1954).

tension between spirit and matter obviously persists. In the regions covered by European languages there is today some agreement to understand by culture "the way of life of a given people", which term embraces all the institutions, customs, faiths, as well as the arts, trades, professions and economic organization of a given people (Dawson). The inner dynamics and basic purpose of culture are seen as tending toward "the unfolding of all that man is potentially capable of" (E. Schillebeeckx).

Yet, history did not bring about cultural uniformity. While every people possesses culture according to the definition of culture just mentioned, it is also a historical fact that these cultures vary. This cultural diversity is today the focal point of interest. Malinowski and A. R. Radcliffe-Brown (functionalism), not satisfied with simple cultural difference, maintained that each culture was an organic whole outside which cultural forms are incomprehensible. In this view, every culture has its own personality or cultural configuration (R. Benedict), which would ensure continuity to the culture as a whole and to its various patterns right through the vicissitudes of history. This view emphasizes the originality of each culture and could preclude any further derivation from ulterior sources. It is also used as a basis for the right of every people to self-development according to its own cultural heritage.

These views, however, lead directly to the complicated problem about the universality and diversity of culture. The right understanding of this question and the nearest possible answer to it are essential to the dialogue between the Church and contemporary cultures.

The overemphasis on the organic character and individuality of a culture may easily lead to a *de facto* understanding of culture as if it were a "nature" (often identified with the character and mentality of a people). Cultural changes and transformations are then easily seen as symptoms of an unhealthy condition. Moreover, the general historical phenomenon of acculturation, cultural formation through the interaction of diverse cultures, becomes then something very problematic. The overall conclusions of history,[8] however, belie any preconceived idea of a rectilinear, predetermined development of cultural subjects. Yet, this idea often influences the views mentioned above.

On the other hand, the concept of the universal aspect of culture is often harmed by a confusion between universalism and uniformity, as if diversity had only a superficial connection with culture. This view is frequently reproached with taking a specific culture, for instance, Western culture, as the criterion by which to judge and fix the norms that must form the basis for development toward a universal culture.

At present, the emphasis on every people's right to express and develop itself according to its own culture is the predominant theme in the study of the relations between the Church and contemporary cultures. Thus, there are numerous studies about how to present the Christian message in a way adapted to the traditional values contained in every cultural system. For missionary problems in general, emphasis is often put on the need to loosen the links with Western culture and to forge a powerful, intimate bond between Christianity and the soul, character and mentality of each people.

In no case should a culture be conceived as static. The incarnation of the message of salvation in the culture of a people, the dialogue between the Church and contemporary cultures, must be firmly rooted in the concrete, living, cultural situation, often difficult to grasp, yet in the continuous development of a human community. It is difficult enough to understand the concrete situation of a small community like a parish. How much more demanding is the insight into a whole cultural system and all its various components.

The definition of the cultural subject, "a People", is not easy either today. No one will deny that today many peoples are in

[8] R. Grousset, *Bilan de l'Histoire* (Plon, Paris, 1946).

a state of formation. One has but to think of the African communities in tension and even in conflict with the traditional tribal groups. This important fact is, moreover, often accompanied by revolutionary changes in the traditional way of life due to the introduction of modern economic and social structures and of modern technological methods.[9] This change in numerous traditional communities is not everywhere the same but is typically brought about by the desire of young communities for equality with the technically more powerful communities, and their wish to occupy a respected cultural place in the international community.

At present the true significance and bearing of the cultural changes now in process can only be outlined in some general observations. Most characteristic is probably the basic change in the relation between the individual person and the community. Where up till now the community dominated, and the family (or clan in the primary group) was in reality the "person", there is now an increasing tendency to stress the individual person as such. This tendency is stimulated by more individual and personal objectives that arise from the acculturation between traditional factors and modern social and economic ones. It is not yet possible to gauge psychological, social and cultural consequences of this process.

This does not, however, prevent the non-Western cultural groups, which are mainly involved in this process, from developing greater self-awareness and self-assertion at the same time. There is a strong tension, if not conflict, between tradition and the demands of the modern community. This is shown, for instance, in the expression "African socialism". It implies a yearning for greater selfhood as well as the yearning for swift social and economic progress. Again, the rationalization of production

[9] P. Verhaegen, "L'Urbanisation de l'Afrique Noire. Son cadre, ses causes et ses conséquences économiques, sociales et culturelles," in *Enquêtes Bibliographiques* (Cedesa, Brussels, 1962).

methods and the distribution of consumer goods implies an escape from a subsistence economy as well as the dismantling of the social structures that belong to this economy. Even values of a religious or of a moral and legal kind are passing through this revolution. On this there are already extensive studies dealing with Africa, Islam, Buddhism, Hinduism, and so on.[10]

Adaptation and "incarnation" in the legitimate individual culture of a people can obviously not encourage a return to the past. This would resemble a binding of Christianity to the vanishing features of culture. It is therefore urgently necessary to establish and maintain the dialogue with those genuine dynamic forces that are at work in the various cultures. The traditions, changes and new developments of each culture must be studied simultaneously. Tradition and new development are today interrelated as rarely before in history.

It would be an illusion to think that what has just been said is only valid for the dialogue with the underdeveloped countries. The dialogue with the civilization of the West (taken historically, not geographically[11]) as a cultural group distinct from the Church, is equally necessary, even though it will be based on different historical data. For this Western culture, too, undergoes the crisis created by tension between traditional and renewal, and here an intensive dialogue must also lead to a constant dynamic adaptation and "incarnation".

In view of the diversity of contemporary cultures and the countless problems that derive from it, we should realize that we are passing through a period of the Church's history in which the diverse contacts between Church and world, between the Church and contemporary cultures, must build the bridge between time and eternity, between humanity and the creator. The understanding of the various cultural groups, constantly deepened

[10] For a summary, see *Weltgeschichte der Gegenwart*, II (Bern, Munich, 1963).

[11] O. H. Simon, "Qu'est-ce que l'Occident?" in *Les Grandes Religions face au Monde d'Aujourd'hui, op. cit.*

by new studies and human contacts, has not only brought out what is valuable in the various ways in which man seeks an existence befitting his human dignity; it also prompts the Church to become better aware of its own nature: to be in the world but not of the world, whether this refers to the Western or the non-Western world.

Finally, dialogue means more than getting into touch with however many various groups. Universal human values are not limited to physical features, but proceed from the unity of a nature that is both material and spiritual and that precedes all diversity. The very basis of this diversity is the human person. Where humanity is concerned, the universal cannot be severed from the diverse. To approach culture as such, without denying or underrating the individuality of each cultural group, is one of the tasks of our time. The deeper insight into the individuality of every culture should lead to a clearer perception of that universally human quality that operates in and through the particularities of every culture. The various cultural patterns lend cohesion to every individual culture, but by the same token they limit or even exclude specific possibilities of development that might lead to the full realization of the human person. When, however, greater awareness of each culture is achieved on a basis as broad and deep as humanity itself, then the way is open for the realization of a genuine universal culture that in no way excludes the true individuality of a particular culture. The unavoidable interaction of various cultures, be it through direct contact or *via* international agencies, will sharpen the awareness of man's true purpose.

This purpose of man is spiritual and religious, and so is the purpose of culture. The dialogue between the Church and contemporary cultures should, therefore, in no way be conceived as a political means of easing the tension between ecclesial and worldly structures. This dialogue ought to encourage also the dialogue between the cultures mutually. As men become more and more aware of their basic unity and their communal purpose, expressed through the diversity of their cultures, they will also better understand the spiritual and religious dimension of the dialogue between the Church and contemporary cultures.

This dialogue between the Church, as the agent of human salvation in living unity with Christ, and a seeking, disunited and swiftly evolving humanity will at the same time influence the Church itself. The renewal and rejuvenation of the Church is not sheer opportunism, but the result of the growing awareness of *her* own nature and her mission in a world that is becoming increasingly conscious of *its* own nature and problems. "When the Church understands herself more and more clearly, and strives to conform to the ideal that Christ put before her, all that distinguishes her from the human situation in which she lives and with which she has to deal, will stand out more clearly. . . . But this distinction does not mean separation. . . . The distinction between the Church and mankind should not lead to opposition but to union. . . . The Church must engage in a dialogue with the world in which she lives."

Not only these quotations, but the whole text of the latest encyclical provide matter for the reflection on the overwhelming task the Church is undertaking by engaging in dialogue with contemporary cultures. This dialogue will have to consider the historical development of mankind. This development is not limited to the past but includes the present and the future. Contemporary cultures as ways of life of different nations contain human values which may, however diversely, lead to the light of faith. These ways of life also include various obstacles to the light of the Spirit. Nevertheless, the dialogue between the Church and contemporary cultures remains the providential instrument for the gift of faith to man, whether individually or communally.

THE INTERNATIONALITY AND VAST SCOPE OF CONCILIUM ARE BEST EVIDENCED BY ITS EDITORS. EACH OF THE THEOLOGICAL AREAS HAS A SPECIALLY APPOINTED GROUP OF EDITORS—MEN WHOSE KNOWLEDGE AND WORK IN THE FIELD ARE KNOWN AND RESPECTED. THE COMPLETE LIST TOTALS NEARLY 300 EDITORS FROM 26 DIFFERENT LANDS.

2. LITURGY

EDITOR
Johannes Wagner — Trier, West Germany

ASSISTANT EDITOR
Helmut Hucke — Rome, Italy

ASSOCIATE EDITORS

Jan van Cauwelaert	Inongo, Congo
Godfrey Diekmann, O.S.B.	Collegeville, Minn., U.S.A.
Balthasar Fischer	Trier, W. Germany
Gaston Fontaine, C.R.I.C.	Montreal, Canada
Adalberto Franquesa, O.S.B.	Montserrat, Spain
Jean Gelineau, S.J.	Paris, France
Anton Hänggi	Fribourg, Switzerland
Denis Eugene Hurley	Durban, South Africa
Henri Jenny	Cambrai, France
Josef Andreas Jungmann, S.J.	Innsbruck, Austria
Emil Lengeling	Münster, West Germany
Frederick R. McManus	Washington, D. C., U.S.A.
Thierry Maertens, O.S.B.	Sint-Andries, Belgium
Salvatore Marsili, O.S.B.	Rome, Italy
Juan Mateos, S.J.	Rome, Italy
Jairo Mejia Gomez	Medellin, Colombia
Ignacio Oñatibia	Vitoria, Spain
Joseph Pascher	Munich, West Germany
George M. Pinell Pons, O.S.B.	Montserrat, Spain
Cyrille Vogel	Strasbourg, France
Cipriano Vagaggini, O.S.B.	Bologna, Italy
Juan Francisco Rivera Recio	Toledo, Spain
Herman A. Schmidt, S.J.	Rome, Italy
Alfred Trusso	Buenos Aires, Argentina
Guilford Clyde Young	Sandy Bay, Australia

3. PASTORAL THEOLOGY

EDITOR
Karl Rahner, S.J.   Munich, W. Germany

ASSISTANT EDITOR
Heinz Schuster   Saarbrücken, W. Germany

ASSOCIATE EDITORS

Ludolph Baas	Amersfoort, Netherlands
Willem van Bekkum, S.V.D.	Surabaya, Indonesia
Joseph Blomjous, P.B.	Mwanza, Tanganyika
Fernand Boulard	Paris, France
Paul Bourgy, O.P.	Brussels, Belgium
Gérard Delcuve, S.J.	Brussels, Belgium
William J. Duschak, S.V.D.	Mindoro, Philippines
Henri Féret, O.P.	Dijon, France
Casiano Floristan	Salamanca, Spain
Domenico Grasso S.J.	Rome, Italy.
Alfonso Gregory	Rio de Janeiro, Brazil
Johannes Hofinger, S.J.	Manila, Philippines
Francois Houtart	Brussels, Belgium
Jésus Iribarren	Madrid, Spain
Jan Kerkhofs, S.J.	Heverlee, Belgium
Francois Lepargneur	São Paulo, Brazil
Pierre-André Liégé, O.P.	Paris, France
Alois Müller	Fribourg, Switzerland
Juan Ochagavia	Santiago, Chile
G. Perez Ramirez	Bogota, Colombia
Emile Pin, S.J.	Rome, Italy
José Rodriguez Medina	Salamanca-Tejares, Spain
Victor Schurr, C.SS.R.	Gars-am-Inn, W. Germany
Emile de Smedt	Bruges, Belgium
Cornelis Trimbos	Utrecht, Netherlands
Manuel Useros Carretero	Salamanca, Spain

4. ECUMENISM

EDITOR
Hans Küng   Tübingen, W. Germany

ASSISTANT EDITORS
Walter Kasper   Tübingen, W. Germany
Hans Joachim Schulz   Münster, W. Germany

ASSOCIATE EDITORS
Charles Alfred Davis   Birmingham, England
Armand Fiolet, O.F.M.   Boxtel, Netherlands
Jan C. Groot   Boxtel, Netherlands
Avery Dulles, S.J.   Woodstock, Md., U.S.A.
Christophe Jean Dumont, O.P.   Boulogne, France
Michael Hurley, S.J.   Dublin, Ireland
Bernard Lambert, O.P.   Quebec, Canada
Joseph Franciscus Lescrauwaet, M.S.C.   Stein, Netherlands
Hendrik van der Linde   Nijmegen, Netherlands
Jorge Mejia   Buenos Aires, Argentina
John M. Oesterriecher   Newark, N. J., U.S.A.
Daniel O'Hanlon, S.J.   Los Gatos, Calif., U.S.A.
Olivier Rousseau, O.S.B.   Chevetogne, Belgium
Thomas Sartory   Munich, W. Germany
Bernhard Schultze   Rome, Italy
Thomas Stransky, C.S.P.   Rome, Italy/Baltimore, Md., U.S.A.
Maurice Villain   Paris, France
Edward D. Vogt   Bergen, Norway
Willem de Vries, S.J.   Rome, Italy
Jan Willebrands   Rome, Italy
Jan L. Witte, S.J.   Rome, Italy
Joacques Yves Marie Lanne, O.S.B.   Rome, Italy
George H. Tavard, A.A.   Pittsburgh, Pa., U.S.A.
Gustave Thils   Louvain, Belgium

5. MORAL THEOLOGY

EDITOR
Franz Böckle

Bonn, W. Germany

ASSISTANT EDITOR
Coen van Ouwerkerk, C.SS.R.

Wittem, Netherlands

ASSOCIATE EDITORS

Reginald Callewaert, O.P. — Louvain, Belgium
Réne Carpentier, S.J. — Egenhoven-Louvain, Belgium
Hervé Carrier, S.J. — Rome, Italy
Philippe Delhaye — Namur, Belgium
G. Gilleman, S.J. — Kurseong, India
Bernard Häring, C.SS.R. — Rome, Italy
Alonzo Hamelin, O.F.M. — Montreal, Canada
Paul Labourdette, O.P. — Toulouse, France
Enda McDonagh — Maynooth, Ireland
Denis Francis O'Callaghan — Maynooth, Ireland
Bernard Olivier, O.P. — Leopoldville, Congo
José Maria Setien — Vitoria, Spain
C. Jaime Snoek, C.SS.R. — Juiz de Flora, Brazil
José Solozabal — Bilbao, Spain
Leonhard Weber — Solothurn, Switzerland
Josef Fuchs — Rome, Italy
Josef Lodewijk Janssens — Heverlee, Belgium

6. THE CHURCH AND THE WORLD

EDITOR
Johan-Baptist Metz

Münster, W. Germany

ASSISTANT EDITORS
Werner Bröker — Münster, W. Germany
Willi Oelmüller — Münster, W. Germany

ASSOCIATE EDITORS

Joseph Comblin — Santiago, Chile
Etienne Cornelis, O.P. — Nijmegen, Netherlands
Adolf Darlapp — München, W. Germany
Heimo Dolch — Beuel-Vilich-Müldorf, W. Germany
Albert Dondeyne — Louvain, Belgium
Gaston Fessard, S.J. — Chantilly, France
Heinrich Fries — Munich, W. Germany
Jean-Yves Jolif — Eveux, France
Joseph Kälin — Fribourg, Switzerland
Andreas M. van Melsen — Nijmegen, Netherlands
Charles Moeller — Louvain, Belgium
Maurice Nédoncelle — Strasbourg, France
Francis O'Farrel, S.J. — Rome, Italy
Max Seckler — Passau, W. Germany
Josef Trütsch — Chur, Switzerland
Jan Walgrave, O.P. — Louvain, Belgium
Bertrand de Clercq, O.P. — Louvain, Belgium
Dominique Dubarle, O.P. — Paris, France

7. THE HISTORY OF THE CHURCH

EDITOR
Roger Aubert   Louvain, Belgium

ASSISTANT EDITOR
Anton Gerard Weiler   Nijmegen, Netherlands

ASSOCIATE EDITORS

Giuseppe Alberigo	Bologna, Italy
Quintin Aldea, S.J.	Comillas, Spain
Justo Fernandez-Alonso	Rome, Italy
Joseph Hajjar	Damascus, Syria
Erwin Iserloh	Trier, W. Germany
M. D. Knowles, O.S.B.	Wimpledon, England
Oskar Köhler	Freiburg, W. Germany
Heinrich Lutz	Scheidt/Saarbrücken, W. Germany
James Patrick Mackey	Belfast, Ireland
Henri Irénée Marrou	Chatenay-Malabry, France
Louis Rogier	Nijmegen, Netherlands
Louis Sala Balust	Salamanca, Spain
John Tracy Ellis	San Francisco, Calif., U.S.A.
Hermann Tüchle	Gröbenzell, W. Germany
Carmelo Juan Giaquinta	Buenos Aires, Argentina

8. CANON LAW

EDITORS

Teodore Jimenez Urresti	Bilbao, Spain
Neophytos Edelby	Damascus, Syria

ASSISTANT EDITOR
Petrus J. M. Huizing, S.J.   Rome, Italy

ASSOCIATE EDITORS

Emanuel Bonet	Rome, Italy
Michael Breydy	Tripoli, Lebanon
Albertus Eysink	Driebergen, Netherlands
Tomas Garcia Barberenà	Salamanca, Spain
Cornelis J. de Jong	Hoeven, Netherlands
Paul Mikat	Düsseldorf, W. Germany
John C. Murray, S.J.	Woodstock, Md., U.S.A.
José Podesta	Avellaneda, Argentina
Robert Soullard	Lyons, France

9. SPIRITUALITY

EDITOR
Christian Duquoc, O.P.   Lyons, France

ASSISTANT EDITOR
Claude Geffré, O.P.   Etiolles, France

ASSOCIATE EDITORS
Bernard Bro, O.P.   Paris, France
Walter Dirks   Cologne, W. Germany
Paul Duployé, O.P.   Strasbourg, France
Henricus Hendrikz   Nijmegen, Netherlands
Marcel Henry, O.P.   Paris, France
Jean Leclercq, O.S.B.   Clervaux, Luxembourg
Joannes Peters, O.C.D.   Smakt-Vernay, Netherlands
Karel Truhlar, S.J.   Rome, Italy
Hans Urs von Balthasar   Basle, Switzerland
Francois Vandenbroucke, O.S.B.   Louvain, Belgium
J. B. Th. van Galen   Aalsmeer, Netherlands
Friedrich Wulf, S.J.   Munich, W. Germany

10. SCRIPTURE

EDITOR
Roland E. Murphy, O. Carm.   Washington, D. C., U.S.A.

ASSISTANT EDITOR
Bas van Iersel, S.M.M.   Nijmegen, Netherlands

ASSOCIATE EDITORS
Barnabas Ahern, C.P.   Rome, Italy
Christopher Butler, O.S.B.   Stratton on the Fosse, England
Jules Cambier, S.D.B.   Leopoldville, Congo
Henri Cazelles   Paris, France
Jacques Dupont, O.S.B.   Bruges, Belgium
André Feuillet, P.S.S.   Paris, France
Joseph A. Fitzmyer   Woodstock, N. Y., U.S.A.
Lucas Grollenberg, O.P.   Nijmegen, Netherlands
Willem M. Grossouw   Nijmegen, Netherlands
Stanislas Lyonnet, S.J.   Lyons, France
Eugène H. Maly   Cincinnati, Ohio, U.S.A.
Franz Mussner   Trier, W. Germany
Karl Hermann Schelkle   Tübingen, W. Germany
Heinrich Schlier   Bonn, W. Germany
Luis Alonso Schökel, S.J.   Rome, Italy
Rudolf Schnackenburg   Würzburg, W. Germany
Heinrich Schürmann   Ehrfurt, W. Germany
Francis Bruce Vawter, C.M.   St. Louis, Mo., U.S.A.
Anton Vögtle   Freiburg, W. Germany